THE CHILD THERAPIST

THE CHILD THERAPIST

PERSONAL TRAITS AND MARKERS OF EFFECTIVENESS

CHRISTIANE BREMS

UNIVERSITY OF ALASKA
ANCHORAGE

Allyn and Bacon
Boston • London • Toronto • Sydney • Tokyo • Singapore

ISBN 0-205-15521-9

Printed in the United States of America

10 9 8 7 6 5 4 3 2 1   98 97 96 95 94 93

CONTENTS

LIST OF TABLES

INTRODUCTION

WHAT THIS BOOK IS ABOUT

INTRODUCTION
WHAT THIS BOOK IS ABOUT

By choosing this book, the reader clearly has made a decision to consider working with child clients. As such a decision is difficult to make and can have many implications, this book was written to help the reader in the decision-making process. This is done in several ways. First, the book will ask difficult questions of the reader that are relevant to her or his training background. Then it will acquaint the reader with the type of personality development and adjustment that is necessary for the effective child therapist. Through this book, the reader will hopefully engage in self-exploration and will gain knowledge that can aid her or him in making a decision about whether becoming a child therapist will be a feasible and desirable professional and personal goal. Providing child therapy can be a very gratifying experience, especially given the odds of improving a child's quality of life. Given findings of a recent meta-analysis of over 100 studies assessing the outcome of child therapy, interventions with children appear to be quite successful (Weisz, Weiss, Alicke, & Klotz, 1987).

Children are a unique therapy population in that all therapists who choose to work with children have childhood as an experience in their own background. It is often claimed that therapists are most successful and empathic in working with those clients who have concerns that the therapist herself or himself has encountered at one point in life. The only population of which it can easily be said that all therapists have experienced life from its perspective is that of children. All therapists have been there; however, having been a child, having children of one's own, or having experienced problems during one's own childhood, does not suffice to qualify a therapist to work with children in

3

psychotherapy, despite the fact that some research indicates that therapists with childhood problems themselves are more effective than those who do not (Poal & Weisz, 1989). There are too many issues to be aware of, too many blind spots unknown about, and too many preconceived notions that may interfere. To think that having been a child will help a therapist understand all children better is just as unrealistic as believing that being a woman automatically makes her a better therapist to work with women, or being a man makes him a better therapist for men. In fact, it is often with exactly the population that the therapist feels a special affinity or understanding that pre-existing attitudes, values, and beliefs can enter the treatment processes in an uncontrolled, unmonitored manner.

Further, even the best training and experience in working with adults will not prepare the therapist for interventions with children. Children are unique and different from adults in a variety of ways that can prove to be quite challenging to the therapist. They are at a different developmental level, and thus have different tasks to master and take different approaches to problem-solving, living, and to the setting of priorities. Their language is not as well-developed, nor is their cognition, emotional expression, or perception. A child therapist not only has to understand these differences from an intellectual, or knowledge, point of view, but also has to realize that these differences alter the type of therapist-client relationship that will develop. Special sensitivities are necessary, and verbal interchanges are no longer primary in the therapy process, as they are in the treatment of adults. Often the therapist has to rely upon nonverbal exchanges to understand the child, to communicate understanding back to the child, to help the child process difficult issues, and to work through difficult transferences. Use of nonverbal communication is often a significant challenge to adults, especially bright and highly educated adults who have been taught for many years that verbal communication is the panacea for most problems that arise.

Consequently, it is extremely important for all therapists interested in working with children to

4

consider a number of important factors before making the final decision to become a child therapist. These are addressed here in several ways. First, the book takes a look at who can become a child therapist from a training, or educational, perspective. Then, the book will explore who can become an effective child therapist from a personal-traits perspective. Finally, a number of issues that are important in the treatment of children will be raised that may have an effect on the therapist's choice about work with this very special population. This discussion of issues is not meant to persuade the reader in one way or another, but merely is included as a warning that work with children is neither as easy as it may seem, nor as difficult! It is meant to provide the best possible backdrop against which the decision of the therapist can be made.

CHAPTER ONE

EDUCATIONAL NEEDS AND BACKGROUNDS OF THE CHILD THERAPIST

CHAPTER ONE
EDUCATIONAL NEEDS AND BACKGROUNDS OF
THE CHILD THERAPIST

There are many professions that can prepare their graduates to become child therapists from a training perspective, obvious ones including psychology, psychiatry, and social work. There is a great variety of job titles that encompass child therapists, and across them exist vast differences in training, experience, and approach. It is impossible to determine which profession best prepares its members to work with children, as most prepare generalists, that is, therapists who supposedly are able to work with any type of client any time. Being trained as a generalist often means that the bulk of the therapist's training experiences has centered around adult clients and adult interventions. While training in various systems of psychotherapy is generally included in the mental health professions that exist, strategies are all too often only applied to adult examples and tried out for the first time with adult clients. This leaves the new therapist unprepared for the work with children and can lead to unsuccessful first attempts at including this clientele in one's caseload. Any therapist trained with adult clients only should receive special supervision for the first child case, regardless of training background. A quick summary of professionals who are considered qualified to provide child mental health services is provided in Table 1.

Obviously, merely having one of these titles is not enough. Course work, reading, training, practical experience, and supervision involving child psychotherapy cases are crucial to successful intervention with this population. Similarly important is a thorough background in and familiarity with child development. It is ultimately the responsibility of each individual mental health service provider to ascertain that she or he has not only adequate credentials to call herself or himself a child therapist, but also adequate background training, experience, and supervision. This supplement only provides the reader with an opportunity to assess her or his readiness to make the choice about whether to become a child therapist. The book which follows it, *A Comprehensive Guide to Child Psychotherapy* (Brems, 1993) is designed to provide the reading background to begin the work with children. However, the success of the reader's application of this material will depend greatly on adequate supervision or consultation if this is the clinician's first attempt at doing therapy with children.

Minimum Training Qualifications for the Child Therapist

The Committee on Professional Standards of the American Psychological Association (APA) and the American Board of Professional Psychology (ABPP) have established standards of minimum qualifications for a number of different aspects of training in psychology, including the practice of psychological assessment, psychotherapy, and neuropsychology (cf., American Psychological Association, 1981, 1985, 1987). Standards and guidelines have also been developed in the literature by individuals or groups of practitioners for relevant practices such as suicide assessments (e.g., Berman, 1990), independent or private practice (e.g., Tuma, 1989), work with women (e.g., American Psychological Association, 1978) and ethnic minorities (e.g., American Psychological Association, 1982), and conduct of growth groups (e.g., American Psychological Association, 1973). Most, if not all, of these guidelines are primarily geared toward and relevant for the adult client. In fact, while special training and practice guidelines exist for adults, nothing of that sort has been written for the work with children. The closest thing in the literature to guidelines relevant to child clients are standards for child abuse assessments (e.g., Skidmore, 1990) and the United Nations' Convention for the Rights of the Child (summarized with regard to their implications for mental health work with children by Wilcox & Naimark, 1991).

Despite this conspicuous absence of standards for the work with children, training programs around the country have begun to recognize the special needs of this population and have made curricular adjustments to prepare clinicians more optimally for intervention with children. Specializations in child clinical work are available at many universities offering doctoral level training in psychology and numerous internship sites. In reviewing curricula of child-sensitive programs and observing child clinical practice, a few minimum requirements emerge that appear necessary for students who plan to engage in child clinical work. These requirements include course work, practical experience, and supervision.

Coursework

Relevant course work that appears minimally necessary includes graduate, that is advanced, training in a number of academic fields. Very importantly, child therapists must have formal course work covering child development. Such coverage should not only focus on traditional theories of development that deal with specific developmental aspects such as cognition, psychosocial and psychosexual stages, motor and language development, or morality (e.g., Bjorklund, 1989; Erikson, 1950; Freud, 1952; Kagan & Lamb, 1987; Piaget, 1967; Whitehurst, 1982), but also non-traditional developmental theories that consider a child's overall self development and interpersonal matrix during the growing-up years (e.g., Chess & Hertzig, 1990; Gerrity, Jones, & Self, 1983; Lane & Schwartz, 1987; Lerner, Skinner, & Sorrell, 1980; Stern, 1977; 1985; 1989).

Formal course work in child psychopathology is indicated as well, as disorders manifest in a variety of

Table 1

Who Can Become A Child Therapist:
A Training Perspective

Career	Degree	Common Title
Psychology		
Counseling	Ph.D., Psy.D.	Psychologist
Clinical	Ph.D., Psy.D.	Psychologist
Child	Ph.D., Psy.D.	Child Psychologist
School	Ph.D., M.S., M.A.	School Psychologist
Counseling	M.S., M.A.	Psychological Associate
Clinical	M.S., M.A.	Psychological Associate
Developmental	Ph.D.	Developmental Psychologist
Counseling		
Counselor Education	Ph.D., Ed.D.	Counselor, Counselor Educator
School Counseling	M.S., M.A., M.Ed.	School Counselor
Counseling	Ph.D., Ed.D.	Counselor

Table 1 Continues

Table 1 Continued

Who Can Become A Child Therapist: A Training Perspective

Career	Degree	Title/License
Social Work		
Clinical Social Work	M.S.W.	Clinical Social Worker
Social Work	B.S.W.	Social Worker
Medicine		
Psychiatry	M.D.	Psychiatrist
Child Psychiatry	M.D.	Child Psychiatrist
Pediatric Psychiatry	M.D.	Pediatric Psychiatrist
Others		
Child Development	M.S., M.A., M.Ed.	Child Development Specialist
Marriage & Family	M.S., M.A.	Marriage & Family Counselor
Juvenile Justice	B.S., B.A.	Juvenile Justice Counselor

different ways at different stages in the lifespan. Further, several disorders occur only in childhood and hence are frequently not covered in sufficient depth and breadth in general psychopathology courses. As an extension of childhood pathology courses, it is also necessary to offer at least one assessment course that is specifically focused on children, without being focused primarily on intellectual, achievement, or cognitive testing. The latter aspects of assessment is often adequately covered for children in general individual assessment courses. However, personality assessment courses need to be focused very differently depending on whether the intended clientele is over or under 18.

A specific course in child therapy is helpful in focusing a trainee's attention toward outcome literature in child psychotherapy, acquainting her or him with the types of interventions that have been used successfully with children. Such a course can also focus attention on specific therapy skills relevant in a child therapy intervention. However, optimally, the research-focused and clinically-focused material would be taught in two separate courses, each covering the separate material in some depth. Clearly such an approach is already common practice in the training of therapists who plan to work with adults. However, adult-focused psychotherapy skills classes are inadequate in helping child-focused trainees gain the exposure to the unique strategies that are used in this setting. For instance, only rarely do traditional therapy skills courses cover story-telling, art, play, or sand tray use.

Finally, a number of supplementary courses would be useful in the preparation of child therapists. All clinicians working with children have to confront the parents of their young clients. These parents are often in desperate need of support and parenting skills training. Hence, coursework in parent eduction and consultation would be extremely helpful to the child clinician. Further, more and more child mental health specialists recognize openly the embeddedness of the child in the family matrix (e.g., Fauber & Kendall, 1992; Moss-Kagel, Abramovitz, & Sager, 1989). Not all

14

children referred for individual therapy are ultimately most likely to benefit from this approach. Often family therapy is the better means of intervention. Hence, the skilled child clinician is also capable of and trained in family therapy. Even if the child therapist has no special expertise in the area of family therapy, all child therapists must have some course work in the area of family assessment, as most child clinicians have moved to an intake model with children that involves the entire family (cf., Brems, 1993).

All child therapists must be knowledgeable about family violence and supplementary coursework must also include domestic violence with a special focus on child abuse and neglect. All therapists working with children must have some basic knowledge about these phenomena with regard to assessment, treatment, ethical implications, and legal issues. Finally, ethical and legal issues do not only arise in a special context for children with regard to interpersonal violence but also in a wide variety of other contexts. Hence, child therapists must receive training in legal issues and ethics facing child therapists, including information about informed consent, search and seizure, release of information, duty to warn and protect, and so on (cf., Brems, 1993).

Practical Experience

It should be obvious by now that becoming a child therapist requires a large number of specially focused courses. However, in addition to information imparted in the academic setting, child therapists must also receive special clinical opportunities during training. Child therapy cases must be part of their practicum and internship case loads. In fact, most optimally, a child therapist will have at least one semester practicum that is entirely focused on children and additional practica that allow for at least some exposure to child clients. Selection of doctoral internships should also be guided by the trainee's desire to work with children. Many internships are available that are entirely focused on children; even more exist that incorporate child work to at least an extent of 50% of a trainee's case load.

While the obvious reason for a child-focused practicum and internship is the exposure to work with children, another advantage is the fact that it is during this time in a person's career that supervision is often freely and generously available. All child therapists must have some supervised experience in working with children. Even therapists who have long graduated and later in their career decide to incorporate children into their caseload need to seek out supervision or intensive consultations as they embark on this venture. Merely having enrolled in a few additional courses (even if all of the courses mentioned above) is not sufficient in training a therapists for the special demands of the work with children.

In summary, working with children is a unique specialty within the mental health field that requires specialized training and practical experience. Training programs exist that provide for these unique needs and requirements. Therapists who are retraining to include children in their case loads have a responsibility to take additional coursework and to gain supervised experience before seeing children on their own. Obviously, as is true for all therapists, the child clinicians' education never ends. Workshops and seminars are excellent continuing education opportunities that can help a child clinician keep up-to-date about the discipline. New developments occur all the time and the responsible clinician will not stop learning and reading. Finally, while the foregoing discussion was clearly most directly focused on psychologists and psychological associates, corresponding courses and experiences are possible and should be required of child clinicians who come from different educational backgrounds.

Settings for the Practice of Child Therapy

In addition to being able to have a variety of educational backgrounds (though similar specific academic and training requirements), child therapists may also practice in a number of greatly divergent settings. Common choices for those professionals at the doctoral level or with a licensable master's degree include, but are not limited to, private practice, community mental health centers, university clinics or counseling centers, medical schools, and hospitals. Child therapists with non-licensable degrees may be found in similar settings, excluding the option for private practice. Ability to bill third-party payors (e.g., insurance companies, Medicaid) depends on credentials of the therapist and/or the therapist's supervisor. Generally, all licensed doctoral-level and some licensable master's level clinicians qualify.

Non-traditional service delivery is also expanding with regard to work with children. More professionals are becoming involved in home-delivery services that are specifically tailored to the needs of the individual child and her or his family and community. Finally, another setting that is unique to the work with children is the school. Child clinicians can work in the role of school counselor or school psychologist. Service delivery in that setting most commonly involves classroom intervention in collaboration with teachers, group interventions that are focused on specific topics (e.g., dealing with parental divorce), and some individual work. Family involvement is rare, though some schools are beginning to conduct topically-oriented groups for parents (e.g., parent education groups).

In summary, work with children can take place in a variety of settings with a variety of different foci, ranging from in-home delivery to group interventions in the school to traditional one-on-one psychotherapy. Regardless of specific treatment focus, child therapists need a basic academic background rounded out with practical experience that is relevant to the final setting in which the clinician plans to practice.

CHAPTER TWO

POSITIVE PERSONAL TRAITS
OF THE CHILD THERAPIST

CHAPTER TWO

POSITIVE PERSONAL TRAITS OF THE CHILD THERAPIST

Despite the wide range of professions and training experiences that prepare the therapist for work with children, the training perspective is still the easier one to discuss when it comes to evaluating who can and cannot be a child therapist. Training is relatively straight-forward, can be evaluated objectively, and can be easily scrutinized by others. However, there are just as many, if not more, personal attributes, expectations, and fears that are either conducive or counterproductive to the work with children. These traits obviously are not as clear-cut, not always possible to evaluate objectively, and not as openly notable by others. The clinician must take the responsibility to evaluate herself or himself along these personality traits. This is often a very difficult and challenging process, as traits are addressed that may not be readily accessible to the therapist's conscious mind. Thus, some trial-and-error learning may have to occur, and some failures may have to be endured by the therapist (and the client) before all of these features are worked out. Despite the difficulty in evaluating these types of characteristics in making a decision about being a child therapist, it is a worthwhile endeavor. The trainee who has difficulty assessing them, may choose to seek some personal therapy or may intensify the amount of supervision received early on in a child case. Looking at the traits that will be discussed here is crucial and should never be omitted, regardless of how tempting that might be. Even if a therapist has worked with adults for several years, evaluation of personal traits is again necessary when children are added to the therapist's caseload. Personal traits are summarized in Table 2.

Common Fears of the Child Therapist

The experienced child therapy supervisor will know that it is not at all uncommon to encounter trainees who are quite afraid of working with children. Working with children mobilizes countertransferences that previously may have gone unnoticed and that never may have been of issue with adult clients. Further, beginning child therapists, especially those trainees without children of their own, often doubt their ability to relate to children on a meaningful level. They are afraid of not being able to communicate, empathize, understand, or interact appropriately. While these concerns are certainly realistic, they are often out of proportion with regard to their actual threat to the therapist's ability to learn to enter into a therapeutic relationship with a child client. It is often helpful for these trainees to begin their work with children in a setting that does not require immediate therapeutic intervention, and thus allows the trainee to become desensitized to being around children, to learn about children's ways of self-expression and children's play, and to recognize developmentally appropriate action.

For instance, one trainee who was very fearful of her required child therapy practicum was first placed in a Head Start classroom (with a supervisor), where she was to observe children, note developmental deficits or advances, evaluate teacher-child interactions, and learn as much about children as possible. After a semester of this indirect interaction with and observation of children, this trainee not only had lost her fear of the work with children, but was looking forward to it. The experience had sufficiently desensitized her to help her recognize that she did not have to become a child to interact with one in a therapeutic manner.

Such a fear of regression to child-like behavior is in fact not uncommon among trainees but generally is unwarranted. The fear of regression itself, however, may affect the therapy in that it may prevent the therapist from being able to recognize immature, perhaps even infantile affects in the child (cf., Bernstein & Glenn, 1988)

22

There is another reason why beginning therapists may choose to work or interact with children in a non-therapy setting first. As Coppolillo (1987) points out, therapy with children should never be (ab)used as an avenue for a (perhaps childless) trainee to find a child to love or with whom to vent parental feelings. Childless trainees are particularly at danger of 'falling in love' with a child client because they may not have contact with children in any other setting. Certainly, the type of interaction and level of sharing encountered in therapy with children will pull parental countertransferences in even the most experienced therapist. However, the therapist who is most at risk of not recognizing these feelings as countertransferential, and hence potentially countertherapeutic, is the one who has not experienced many contacts with children and may not recognize that this affect or attitude must not always be a component of the child-therapist relationship. Thus, some supervisors of beginning child therapists recommend that young therapists who do not have children of their own to love, volunteer for work with children in a non-therapeutic role (e.g., Big Brothers/Big Sisters) to deal with emerging parental affects in that setting (Coppolillo, 1987).

Other fears that are at times mentioned by child therapist trainees are fears of not being able to cope with children who have and express strong feelings, inability to set appropriate and safe limits in case a child begins to act out aggressively and behaviorally, overidentification and emotional overinvolvement with the child if she or he discloses abuse or neglect, strong feelings toward abusive or neglectful parents, and lack of aptitude for communicating without words (cf., Bernstein & Glenn, 1988). While all of these fears have a grain of truth and reality, most trainees exaggerate their response to them. All of the situations that are stimuli for a trainee's fears can be handled effectively as long as the therapist has received some training and guidelines about how to intervene. In other words, simply receiving child therapy training generally suffices to desensitize the therapist in training to these fears, as she or he begins to recognize that their proportion is not realistic given the tools of trade that are available to deal with each specific feared situation.

Common Expectations of the Child Therapist

Often, beginning therapists expect all children with whom they will work are going to be lovable and vulnerable. They are then taken by surprise and thrown off balance by the tough child who fails to evoke feelings of caring and concern in the therapist. However, it is a reality that it is often exactly these children who find their way into the therapy room as they are the ones most easily identifiable as in need of treatment. Yet, they are also the children who have learned to harden themselves against adult intervention as a matter of self-protection and as a reaction to an often very emotionally deprived environment. The novice therapist tends to be overwhelmed by the harshness of these children's overt behavior and communication, and has difficulty recognizing these overt manifestations of emotional pain as what they are: signs of psychic pain and desperate cries for help. Thus, beginning therapists have difficulty establishing a meaningful relationship with such a child, and are often disillusioned about their ability to connect with children in general. However, with some help from a supervisor, these trainees can learn to recognize the child's behavior for what it is, and can often establish an understanding bond with the child. They may never 'love' this child, because she or he may never be the sweet or lovable person that was expected. However, almost always are therapists able at least to recognize one feature in the child with which they can connect and through which a therapeutic interaction can develop and grow.

Positive Attributes of the Child Therapist

Regardless of educational background, and no matter what is feared or expected, therapists' effectiveness is perhaps most closely tied to personal traits that will affect the relationships between child and therapist. Chrzanowski (1989, p. 600) describes therapy as a "relational contact with a shared goal", emphasizing that personality of the therapist plays a critical role in how therapy will progress. Clearly 'personality' is a rather vast and ill defined variable and it is difficult to describe a type of personality that would lend itself better or worse for therapeutic work. However, personality can be broken down into relatively simple, perhaps even objective traits, which, in turn, can be identified as related to more or less success in the treatment effort with children. Several such personality traits have been identified in the literature and each will be briefly discussed here. Certainly, the list of traits provided here may not be all-inclusive; however, it presents some of the more critical aspects of the successful child therapist's characteristics.

Self-Respect and Self-Esteem

The challenges of the difficult child described earlier hopefully serve to clarify why the beginning child therapist must bring to treatment a healthy dose of self-respect and self-esteem. Early interactions with difficult children are often extremely taxing for the therapist's self-esteem as all empathic and reflective skills that tend to work even with the most difficult adults may be lost on challenging children (if not only because these skills rely very heavily on verbal communication, an avenue not always usable in the work with children). Even when faced with such a potential failure or difficulty, the therapist must be able to maintain a sense of self-respect and esteem to remain efficient and capable in her or his work. Self-esteem and self-respect are crucial even in the work with children who have less challenging symptoms. Deficits in the therapist's self-confidence result in her or his needs to have a child client perform in a specific manner to validate for the therapist that she or he is a good clinician. Any deviations from the "good-client" role by

Table 2

Positive Attributes of the Child Therapist

----

* acceptance of that not all children are 'lovable'
* lack of fear of children
* self-respect and self-esteem
* self-awareness and willingness for self-
    exploration
* open-mindedness about values, behaviors, and
    approaches to life
* restraint from imposing own values, standards,
    or beliefs
* cultural and gender sensitivity
* awareness of the impact and manifestation of
    prejudice
* use of non-offensive, non-sexist, and non-racist
    language
* respect for child's needs and wishes
* respect for child's privacy and confidentiality
* acceptance of child's definition of what is
    important
* awareness of child's cognitive level and
    limitations
* adaptability to child's level and style of
    functioning
* knowledge and understanding of symbolism and
    metaphor
* empathy and willingness to listen
* tolerance for ambiguity and tentativeness
* truthfulness to one's self
* awareness of personal style
* compatibility of personal style with chosen
    therapeutic style
* awareness of dress and other aspects of
    appearance
* appropriate clothing to prevent injury or offense
* respect for and acceptance of child's parents
* willingness to seek consultation

----

the child is perceived as a threat to the therapist's professional self-esteem and may result in interventions that are inappropriate. Thus, self-esteem and self-respect are crucial to avoiding the use of the child for one's own purposes or psychological needs.

Why would this be so important in the work with children as opposed to work with adults? While lack of self-esteem in the therapist can threaten any therapeutic relationship, it is a particular challenge to the relationship with the child because, as an adult, the therapist is more likely to expect conformity and obedience from a child than from another adult. As an adult, the therapist has generally encountered a sufficient number of interchanges with other adults by which or whom she or he was challenged or opposed. However, these experiences are much less likely to have occurred outside the therapy setting with children, as children do tend to respond with respect to adult strangers. Thus, misconduct or unexpected behavior on the part of the child can present a great challenge to the self-esteem of the novice therapist.

For instance, one very new therapist was extremely distraught after his second session with a child client. This trainee had previously experienced some difficulty with his adult clients, showing some limits in empathic potential and often feeling the need to convince his clients that they were already doing much better than when they entered treatment. The therapist had been made aware by his supervisor that there was a likely connection between his need to perceive progress and his significant doubts about his own competence. However, this connection became even clearer after his first two sessions with his child client.

The child, being referred for oppositional behavior, had consistently refused to listen to directives (the appropriateness of which certainly was also in question) given by the therapist. It became clear upon viewing the tape of the session that the trainee became more and more exasperated and finally no longer knew what to do. At that time he literally begged the child to behave, as otherwise he (the therapist) would not receive a good grade in his practicum! Clearly, not all examples of low self-esteem will end up surfacing in a manner quite this obvious. But self-doubts have a way of showing themselves in treatment with children, if only in subtle ways that communicate to the child that the therapist is not really strong or in control.

Self-Awareness

It should be quite obvious by now that the child therapist must possess a high level of self-awareness and maturity, lest all sorts of confounding feelings and attitudes may enter into the treatment process (cf., Knobel, 1990). Self-awareness again is a therapist trait that is important in the work with all clients regardless of age (Chrzanowski, 1989; Chung, 1990). Yet, it is of particular importance in the work with children because this interaction often pulls for countertransferences and affects that are a part of the therapist's own very early life. Thus, the feelings that are evoked are often raw affects that have not been sufficiently processed, or that the therapist has not experienced in many years. The younger the child, the more deeply buried the material that is evoked in the therapist (Chethik, 1969). Lack of awareness of early-life countertransferential desires or needs can result in feelings of being startled, overwhelmed, or confused.

Additionally, children tend to be experienced by the therapist as much more vulnerable than adult clients. Thus, therapists who have a caretaker stance that can be controlled quite well in the work with adults, may not be able to control this need in the work with children. Further, children are even more likely than adults to ask for direct advice or guidance, making it even more difficult for the beginning therapist not to fall into the trap of becoming an advice-giver or teacher (Siegel, 1990). This is a common problem for novice therapists anyhow, as they tend to think that they should have answers for clients; that they should be able to deliver an obvious service or product. This attitude is in line with Western society that stresses measurable and observable contributions or products, as opposed to valuing interactions that are designed to support, convey understanding, and aid in self-exploration. Thus, the novice Westernized therapist is often very disturbed when she or he recognizes that therapy does not deliver a product, but rather provides an atmosphere that facilitates growth and change. She or he tends to belittle the work that is being done because of the absence of a tangible result after each individual session. While in the treatment of adults, the novice can sometimes overcome this feeling by producing a verbal session summary or by developing a gauge with which to measure the client's progress, this is much more difficult to do in the treatment with children.

For example, one trainee who was working under supervision was quite distraught after the third week of work with a child client because, according to her, nothing was happening in the treatment of this 12-year old. In exploring the last session with this girl, it became very obvious to the supervisor that indeed this child was beginning to experience a significant level of trust in the therapist and was beginning to open up and to 'work on' several important therapeutic family issues. The novice therapist had not been able to see this progress because the child did not complete a project begun during the session, failed to engage in much verbal interchange (despite her advanced age), and indicated that she was getting bored being with the therapist. The client's expression of boredom occurred, however, after she had spontaneously begun drawing a picture of her family. In this picture, her father was an imposing and very large figure in the middle of the page, her brother was next to him, also quite large, and the client herself was in a corner of the drawing, very small and without elaboration. While drawing, the client indicated that her brother tended to get all the attention since the parental divorce because her mother was afraid that he was not receiving sufficient male role-modeling because the male parent was no longer living with the family. In an attempt to make this up to the brother, the mother had been focusing many of her energies onto this child, leaving her two daughters to their own devices.

The child never previously had indicated that she felt affected by her parents' divorce, instead indicated that she felt quite relieved by it. This was the first sign that she indeed was affected significantly and was ready to share this with her therapist. However, she abandoned the drawing at this point, turned to her therapist and claimed she was bored. The therapist, concerned about her inability to keep the client engaged, perceived this session as a failure because of the lack of a product that resulted. Once she was able to recognize that her own needs for tangibles had interfered in her ability to make a realistic assessment of her session, she felt much more comfortable about her impending next session with this child.

Open-Mindedness

Self-awareness is an important trait and it often brings with it another important characteristic of the child therapists, namely, open-mindedness (Stadler, 1985). The more self-aware a therapist is, the less she or he is threatened by differentness of a child and her or his family, by obstinacy of a client, and by what appear to be temporary and occasional treatment failures. The open-minded therapist will welcome a child who has values that differ from her or his own and will not force personal values onto the child. This is especially important if the child grew up in an environment that was significantly different from that of the therapist, as is often the case. Unfortunately, the bulk of therapists today have middle class backgrounds, whereas the bulk of child clients tends to come from more disadvantaged socioeconomic strata. These differences in background are likely to have forged different sets of values and priorities for child and therapist. This difference will not threaten treatment as long as the therapist can keep an open mind, in other words, is able to see the child's life from the child's unique perspective. Thus, what the therapist may need to understand is that some behaviors of the child that would have been considered maladaptive or at least questionable in the therapist's background, may have great adaptive value in the child's environment.

For instance, one trainee had grown up in a family in which expression of emotion was extremely desirable and in which the parents encouraged their children to speak about feelings even if they were negative or oriented against the parent. This approach worked very well for the problem-solving process in this particular family. Subsequently, this therapist endorsed free communication of affect as an important therapeutic goal in his treatment of clients. However, as he came to recognize very painfully, this standard could not be realistically upheld with several of his child clients. In one case in particular, the free expression of affect by the child subsequent to one session that had utilized story-telling as a primary intervention strategy, almost led to physical abuse of the child by the mother. This family was clearly not ready to incorporate the trainee's value system about the usefulness of affective expression or honesty. This example clarifies also that a child is embedded in an interpersonal matrix that may not always change with the child, regardless of the strides that the client is making in treatment. Teaching the child values or standards that are not part of her or his family values and standards will inevitably lead to conflicts between the child and her or his parents. It is important for the therapist to proceed cautiously and to be very aware of the family's values and standards.

Finally, the therapist may never assume that she or he knows what is right or wrong for a given family. The adaptiveness of their values and beliefs must be explored given their unique environment and history. Therapy is no place for rigid value judgment. Rather, it is a place for flexibility and willingness to see things in a manner that maximizes options and choices, while ascertaining that they are adaptive and useful for the psychological growth and _safety_ of the child (cf., Muslin & Val, 1987). Clearly, neither science nor art (and therapy is generally considered to contain both) can be entirely free of values and value judgments (Lewis &

Walsh, 1980). However, the therapist is encouraged to be as flexible and open-minded as possible, and to recognize own values and how they may collide with the values of a client and family. In other words, while therapists may be unable to refrain from some value judgments, they must learn about their own values in order not to allow them to cloud the work that needs to be done (Graham, 1980).

Cultural and Gender Sensitivity

Open-mindedness about values and standards is also implied in the therapist's need for sensitivity to ethnic differences. Children come from a variety of ethnic backgrounds, all of which differ slightly in their interpersonal emphasis, affective expression, understanding of human life, priorities for living, and other aspects of being human (Gibbs & Huang, 1989). The therapist must be willing to explore the child's background to understand fully from where she or he is coming and to where she or he will return after a session is over or therapy is complete.

It is important to keep in mind that while there is significant variation across ethnic groups, there is also significant variation within each ethnic group (Johnson, 1993). That is to say that the therapist should never assume that because a child is from a certain ethnic group, she or he will display certain attitudes or behaviors. This attitude, often misunderstood as cultural sensitivity, is actually the worst manifestation of prejudice there is. Sensitivity to cross-cultural differences is a must; however, it is not to be used as a way of organizing or categorizing people along certain dimensions! There is uniqueness in every family, whether it is Asian American, African American, or European American. No therapist would ever assume that all White children's families have the same structure. However, it is unfortunately still common to hear therapists talk in such global terms about children's families from other ethnic backgrounds.

One example of stereotyping confused with cultural sensitivity occurred during a child's case staffing after a lengthy intake with a therapist with significant experience. During the course of the presentation, this therapist indicated that the presenting family was completely run and organized by the child's mother, adding to the comment that this was to be expected as the child was African American. Several clinicians who had listened to his presentation were quite surprised by his conclusions, as in actuality it was the father who had brought the family to treatment, the father who was caring for the children (he was unemployed, the mother worked), and it was the father whom the children sought out for problem-solving! In the therapist's attempt to be culturally sensitive, he actually imposed his own stereotypes about Black culture onto this family to such a degree that he let it override the evidence that had been presented to him by this (actually very well-functioning) family. Thus, the beginning therapist must juggle her or his desire to know as much about each ethnic group in general with the need to be open-minded and enter each intake interview without preconceived notions regarding what to expect.

Obviously, though, the novice therapist must also learn to monitor her or his language to avoid sexism, racism, or other offensive language. Despite much education in recent years, sexism is alive and well in the mental health field. This reality has frequently been documented for the work with adults, but also has affected therapy with children (Schweid, 1980). Sexism, however obvious or subtle, is important for the novice to investigate as it is not uncommon for even the most aware and sensitive individual to have ingrained language patterns that are not meant to offend, yet do. Thus, the use of words that incorporate 'man' supposedly as the generic designation for 'human', such as fisherman, businessman, congressman, or mankind, should be avoided. This avoidance is recommended not only to prevent offending the adult women in a family that presents for an intake interview, but also to prevent subtle messages from reaching young children who are seen in treatment.

Consider the therapist working with a young girl who is quite withdrawn or unsure of herself. This sexist language will no doubt contribute to her view of herself as passive, as unable to reach many goals in life because they are reserved for men, and as not in control of her own destiny. Sexism can occur also in the choice of activities, toys, or rules set in the therapy room. The beginning therapist needs to recognize her or his own stereotypes about what is deemed appropriate for boys versus girls. In actuality, every activity available in the room, every rule ever made in treatment, and every statement uttered by a therapist should be applicable to boys and girls alike. Even the most subtle influences over the child's behavior that are sex-role stereotyped can have long lasting effects.

Avoidance of offensive language and awareness of stereotypes is equally important in the context of ethnic differences. If a therapist is not sure about a child's culture, reading about it is not enough. The family needs to be asked what being Asian American means to them and how they perceive their culture. It never pays to pretend to understand a family's cultural background completely, and it is much more honest and conducive to rapport-building to ask questions and to clarify information given a family's cultural history. Similarly, sensitivity to level of acculturation is extremely important, and this too can only be adequately assessed by asking direct and honest questions (Dillard, 1983). Racism and sexism in language and behavior also must be avoided even if the child or family use this language or behavior. Even in reflecting a child's feelings, the therapist has the responsibility to help the family recognize that ethnic or gender prejudices are not part of her or his repertoire (cf., Johnson, 1993). Thus, if a child in therapy uses offensive language, the therapist may reflect her or his feeling, but must substitute the appropriate term. In other words, the child's use of words such as Jap, nigger, wetback, and so forth, never justifies the use of such expressions by the therapist!

Of course these cautions about sexism and racism are in no way to imply that a therapist cannot work with a family of a different cultural background or with a child of the opposite sex. An African American therapist can do a wonderful job with a Mexican-American child; there is no doubt about that. These cautions are merely meant to raise awareness and sensitivity about these issues in an attempt to help the therapist note her or his own prejudices and to make the world a little fairer place to live in, in general.

Respect for the Child

Also relevant to open-mindedness and sensitivity, is the therapist's respect for the child's sense of what is and is not important. In his book, Coppolillo (1987) provides a beautiful example of scheduling his treatment around a child client's favorite TV show. Another therapist challenged Coppolillo's action, but as he points out, a child's play is a child's work. Therapists rarely require an adult client to cancel a business appointment if it can easily be avoided by scheduling her or his session at a different time. Why should this courtesy not be extended to children? Children do have lives of their own, important preferences, and a clear understanding of what they want and do not want. Forcing a child to come to treatment at a certain time or to engage in specific behaviors without considering the child's preferences lacks respect and opens the door for unnecessary resistances.

Respect for a child also includes respecting her or his privacy and confidentiality! Therapists would not even have to be warned about the many ways in which they violate children's confidentiality if they were dealing with adult clients. How many therapists expecting an adult client would enter the waiting area, asking "Are you Mary Simmons?" Yet, numerous therapists violate this easily avoidable breach of confidentiality with children. How many therapists would tell an adult client's curious parent what the client said about her in the last session? How many therapists of an adult client (even with a release-of-information) would divulge specifics about the client's therapy to a concerned mother? Yet all of these behaviors are sometimes displayed by therapists of children. They violate children's rights and show a lack of respect for children's confidentiality that can easily undermine treatment.

Respect for the child also means being aware of what is and is not comfortable for the child. One example of that type of respectful sensitivity has to do with physical touch. While physical touch is not in and of itself good or bad, the context in which it occurs and the communication it expresses can render it unhealthy and demeaning or therapeutic and respectful. If touch is used by a therapist to communicate an atmosphere of caring and safety, it can prove quite beneficial to therapy (Kupfermann & Smaldino, 1987). However, if touch is always negative (e.g., only occurs in the context of restraining the child) it may prove countertherapeutic. Regardless of the intention, however, physical touch is only appropriate if the child is comfortable with it and not threatened by it. A therapist must respect a child's physical boundaries and may not invade them if the child communicates that touch is not desired.

Another issue that arises in the context of respectful interactions with children has to do with habits of the therapist. Any habit that is unhealthful to the child is inappropriate for the therapist to engage in while with the child. For instance, one hopefully unnecessary caution in this regard is the fact that children are not used to asking adults to change their behavior even if it causes them distress. Thus, an adult therapist should never smoke around a child client. Nor should she or he put the child in the position of granting the therapist permission to do so. In other words, while it may be (marginally) acceptable to ask an adult client whether she or he would be bothered by the therapist's smoking, a child should never even be asked the question because it is not clear whether the child would have the courage to turn the therapist down (it is not even clear that all adult clients would have this ego strength). The clinician has to respect the child enough not even to put the child in such a compromising position.

Two final issues that must be raised within the category of respect for the child are the therapist's efforts to understand the child given her or his developmental level and to communicate with the child through metaphor. Children, especially young children, have vastly different ways of thinking than adults. Their cognitive processes are less flexible and logical and their reasoning is relatively concrete. A therapist must be willing to use language and explanations that make sense to the child at the child's developmental level. A therapist must not assess developmental level based on the child's age, but rather on interactions with the child designed to assess the child's actual developmental (not chronological) age. Given the importance of this issue it is further addressed in a subsequent chapter.

The use of metaphor and symbolism is very important in the work with children. Children do not necessarily communicate through direct verbal expression, at least in part because they may be lacking the necessary language skills. A child therapist hence must make an effort at coming to understand the child's use of metaphor and symbolism in order to understand fully her or his communications with the therapist. Again, given the importance of this issue to the therapy process, it is discussed in some detail in a subsequent chapter.

Empathy and Willingness to Listen

All therapies are concerned with the therapist's ability to empathize with a client. It is critical that the child therapist have the ability to look at life from the unique perspective of the child. It is not sufficient that the therapist understand how she or he would feel or would have felt if she or he were in the child's shoes. Instead, the therapist must understand how the child feels in a given situation, given that child's specific and unique experiences, history, and background (cf., Kohut, 1984). Empathy, thus defined, requires the therapist to listen carefully and to hear or see not only the overt content of what is being expressed either verbally or behaviorally, but also to listen to the more latent message that is contained within the child's expression. Such empathy, also termed vicarious introspection (Kohut & Wolf, 1978), is not the warm, fuzzy feeling of caring, but rather is an artful and scientific approach to better understanding.

Empathy is also incomplete if it ends with the internal or private understanding of the child by the therapist. Empathy only serves a positive therapeutic purpose if the therapist is able to communicate her or his understanding back to the child. In other words, once the therapist has listened carefully and believes she or he has empathically understood the communication of the child, this understanding must somehow be communicated back to the child. Only when the child receives this message of understanding and feels the therapist's empathic concern is the interpersonal cycle of empathy considered to be complete (cf., Barrett-Lennard, 1981; Brems, 1989a). The need to communicate empathy to the child, however, is not to be misunderstood as verbalizing understanding or making an interpretation. It can often be communicated just as easily through nonverbal media; for instance, by joining a child's play or by matching one's affect to the child's (also refer to Stern, 1984). It may be as simple as joining in a child's laughter, sharing a child's delight, or recognizing a child's fears and providing support. Or it may be a complex process of interaction that involves thorough understanding of child, therapeutic medium, and metaphor.

An example of a more sophisticated empathic cycle is provided by this brief vignette of a child-therapist interaction. A ten-year old girl was referred for treatment of nightterrors which had been increasing in frequency over the past four months. She was engaged in a rather successful therapy with a therapist with considerable experience in her work with children.

Toward the middle phase of treatment, this child told the following story:

> Once there was a little house. This little house had many many rooms and a big attic and a basement. The house liked all its room but was very afraid of going in the basement because down there lived a big ugly looking monster animal. The monster animal was always awake because it could not sleep. The house didn't like the monster animal so it didn't go to the basement. One day it had to go down there because it needed potatoes to eat. And the big ugly monster came out an roared at the little house. The house ran as far away as it could but it never forgot the monster animal - after that it made sure never that it never goes to the basement.

The therapist listened to the story and given what she knew about the girl understood her communication. The girl had often sought to receive more nurturance from her parents who were rather rigid and strict people who showed little emotion and caring. One time, after the girl had felt particularly lonely and frightened after a nightmare, she had crawled into her parents' bed. Rather than comforting the child and asking why she had come into their bedroom, both parents responded with rage. After that time, the little girl had never returned to her parents' bedroom and had apparently given up seeking emotional (or other types of) help from them. Understanding the girl's communication, the therapist responded as follows:

> The little house got so scared because all it wanted was some potatoes. It did not mean to upset the basement or the monster animal - it's just that it was so hungry. Now the little house is so scared of the monster animal that is doesn't even want to come close to it. The problem is that that's where the potatoes are. So now the little house is all confused and scared! What was it going to do now?

The little girl began to cry and it was clear that the therapist had communicated her understanding correctly. The two then began to problem-solve about what the little house could do to be fed without the fear of being hurt by the monster. This example clarifies the power of empathy, as well as the power of remaining within the child's metaphor, rather than communicating understanding concretely. In other words, the therapist's empathic understanding would not have been nearly as successful, had she tried to make the latent content (i.e., the metaphor) manifest.

Flexibility and Tolerance of Ambiguity

Respect and empathy for the child as well as sensitivity to a child's gender or ethnic background all imply that the therapist cannot treat all children alike (Adams, 1982). Similarly, the same child cannot forever be treated the same way. Children change; so do their systems and presenting concerns. To remain ever aware of these changes requires tolerance and flexibility, two traits that are important for other reasons as well (Knobel, 1990). Specifically, in all therapies, but especially in the treatment of children, new information constantly emerges as work progresses. This results in constant revisions of treatment plans and conceptualizations, and requires adaptability of treatment strategies in a meaningful and planful manner. Not all human beings are capable of functioning in such an environment of ambiguity and tentativeness. Not a few will attempt to make the therapy fit a rigid model, forcing the understanding of the child into a mold. This is a dangerous lack of flexibility that can cause stagnation at best, iatrogenesis at worst. No child, no family, no therapy fits a specific mold. In fact, the whole therapeutic process relies upon change, upheaval, tentativeness, and not uncommonly, ambiguity.

For a therapist, it is important to be able to deal with unknowns and to be willing to take risks and explore new grounds. All child therapists have to be capable of "epistemological feeling" (Knobel, 1990, p. 61), that is, they must have the ability to listen empathically and to alter their assessments of a child's situation flexibly and appropriately to changing contexts. Unwillingness to follow intuitions can result in leaving facets of the child undiscovered that may otherwise prove crucial to her or his growth and change. Certainly, this risk-taking has to be weighed against the possible consequences of making a mistake. However, it is rare that one failed or inappropriate treatment intervention will derail the entire therapeutic process. In fact, some clinicians believe that the occasional empathic failure of the therapist is crucial to successful treatment (Kohut, 1984). It is often much more preferable for the therapist to risk a new intervention than to adhere rigidly to one that is clearly unsuccessful. Repeated failures are likely to be more impactful than one unfortunate choice of wording or behavior.

Being True to One's Self

In intervening in the therapy process with a child, it is important that the therapist allow her or his own self to come through and to be truly authentic (Knobel, 1990). It is generally quite impossible for a clinician to deny how she or he really is outside of the therapy room. Personality can neither be hidden nor should it be camouflaged (Chrzanowski, 1989). Yet, authenticity does not imply that the therapist engage in self-disclosure. Absolutely not! The therapy is there for the child, not for the therapist to self-disclose or deal with her or his own psychological or emotional issues. However, all therapists have a personality and an interpersonal style (so one would hope, at least). Some are extroverted and active; others are introverted and observing. This general pattern shows through in the type of treatment a clinician chooses (cf., Keinan, Almagor, & Ben-Porath, 1989; Kolevzon, Sowers-Hoag, Hoffman, 1989). Thus, it is unreasonable for the active, extroverted therapist to expect to engage in the type of play therapy that Virginia Axline (1947) conducts. She or he would find herself or himself denying an aspect of the self that would keep trying to slip through and would interrupt the treatment process. This therapist would be much better suited for a more interactive model of play or activity therapy.

Thus, as the beginning therapist searches for her or his way of conducting psychotherapy with children, her or his own personality needs to be considered, accepted, and used to the person's advantage. Trying to deny who one is never works for any length of time. Finding a way of doing therapy that fits with the therapist's general style of being and with her or his life values is worth the effort. Only if the style fits the clinician will she or he be able to muster the enthusiasm that is so crucial to the treatment of any client. A bored therapist is indeed a difficult one to picture as successful in instilling a sense of enthusiasm and challenge in the child.

A note of caution is necessary here. While being true to one's self is important as personal traits will come through whether intended or not, there are some personality traits that are likely to be counterproductive in the work with children. Such traits include excessive formality, rigidity, intolerance of getting dirty or messy, arrogance vis-a-vis children, selfishness, lack of awareness of safety limits, and similar characteristics. While any and all of these traits may express the true being of the therapist, they are nevertheless not appropriate if expressed in child therapy. In fact, presence of any of these traits makes it questionable whether the given individual should be a child therapist (or a mental health professional in general) at all!

Awareness of Dress

Regardless of personal style, there are some cautions about dress that even the most formal therapist needs to consider (e.g., Webb, 1989). A rule of thumb in the work with children is neither to wear a tuxedo (Ginott, 1964), nor to wear clothing that is entirely outside the cultural norms of the society within which the clinician practices. This leaves plenty of leeway in terms of choices, but a few more cautions are necessary. For instance, there is some agreement that overly formal dress can impede the establishment of rapport (Barker, 1990). Further, children will show affection spontaneously without regard to whether fingers are clean or dirty (Coppolillo, 1987). Thus, wearing clothes that cannot be easily washed is a set-up for anger or hostility on the part of the therapist in response to what was meant to be a positive interaction by the child. In other words, the therapist should be willing to let the clothes get dirty. Of course this does not mean that there are no rules in the therapy room. Indeed there are; however, harmless and occasional violations, accidents, or spontaneous shows of affection should not become great problems in the child-therapist relationship. Aside from clothing, therapists also need to use common sense about jewelry, scarfs, neck ties, high-heeled shoes, and similar accessories that can be used to hurt, either purposefully or accidentally. Women need to decide whether wearing a skirt will make them uncomfortable in situation where they may have to sit on the floor, climb on a chair, or engage in similar activities that may result in potential embarrassment, lack of comfort, preoccupation with one's clothing, or even injury. Clearly, therapeutic style will have some impact on choice of clothing.

Another feature of the child therapy setting that may impact choice of dress and jewelry is that of the child's own socioeconomic background. Some clinical settings are in neighborhoods or have catchment areas that are of lower socioeconomic status than the therapist may be part of. Before putting on expensive clothing or obvious jewelry, the therapist may need to consider the impact of this behavior on the client. A child who may not always be adequately nourished may have significant difficulty trusting a therapist who because of dress or jewelry (from the child's or parents' perspective) so obviously will not understand this very basic physical concern.

An example of the impact of expensive jewelry is the case of a small boy who was to be seen by a therapist in training of upper middle class background.

This therapist was a very beautiful woman who dressed stylishly in expensive clothing and wore valuable jewelry. She often wore several rings, as well as necklaces and bracelets. Her attire had previously surfaced in supervision, but not with much emphasis or consequence. However, the issue finally needed to be dealt with very obviously when this therapist began to work with a small boy who had been born to very poor parents who were having significant difficulties making ends meet.

This child was presented because of depression that was rather chronic. He had begun treatment four months with a male trainee who quickly made great strides in the child's treatment. When he graduated, the small boy and he had a termination "party" when they shared food provided by the therapist. The subsequent week, the child was introduced to the new therapist described above. Despite having been well prepared for the transfer, he began to cry softly upon being invited to the therapy room. With some coaxing he was finally willing to enter the session. He did not engage well in play and the therapist was getting quite desperate. She tried many means of building rapport but the child was unable to connect with her.

When the tape of the session was reviewed, both supervisor and therapist noted the child's obvious preoccupation with the therapist's hands. He stared at them and seemed to respond to gestures by the therapist by becoming further upset. Both clinicians began to hypothesize that he was upset by the therapist's jewelry. A conference with his parents revealed that one area of frequent argument was money and that most recently the couple had to sell the wife's wedding band. This led to many ill feelings in the spousal relationship. The therapist entered the next session feeling less sophisticated (as she wore less fancy clothes and no jewelry), but the child rewarded her by becoming more willing to engage in therapeutic activities. The transfer remained difficult; but some of the tension was reduced once an obvious hindrance to rapport for the child had been eliminated by the therapist.

Respect for the Child's Parents

While tolerance and understanding for the child client have already been stressed, the same basic attitudes and feelings must be extended to the child's parents. The therapist must maintain the ability to keep track of the parents' perspective as well as the child's (cf., Brems, 1993). It is very easy to forget that parents too are in pain, even if they are abusing or neglecting their child. It is important for the therapist to muster empathy even for the most inappropriate parent, as one reason this parent behaves so dismally toward the child may be that she or he also has significant psychological or emotional deficits, unmet needs, or concerns. Often the parents of abused children were abused themselves and are in dire need of treatment themselves (Ammerman & Hersen, 1992). Regardless of the overt resistance that they may show, their pain, however deeply buried, needs to be kept in mind by the clinician to ascertain that adequate empathy and understanding is extended to the parent (Brems, Baldwin, & Baxter, 1993). Angry or hostile confrontations by the therapist may only serve to alienate the parent which may lead to a premature termination of services for the child. It is not uncommon for the novice therapist to express strong negative feelings, sometimes even disgust, about abusive parents. Such an attitude will not help the treatment process and the therapist must gain control of these countertransferential feelings.

Sometimes the best way to address negative countertransference toward parents is through being assigned as the therapist for one of the parents, not the child. This will give the new therapist a chance to look at the parent's background and childhood history. This generally helps the therapist recognize the tragedy of the parent's life that has led her or him to the point of being an abusive individual. If the trainee is so repelled by the abusive parent as to not be able to work with her or him in a therapeutic relationship, it is strongly advised that she or he seek supervision or consultation regarding this matter. No child therapist can work with children without encountering the abusive or neglectful parent. Inability to establish rapport or a positive interaction with such a parent will get in the way of successful treatment of the child. Parents are critical to the therapy of children; they bring them, they control when a child comes and how often a child comes, they are generally responsible for payment, and they decide whether therapy is working. Alienating them can short-circuit the chance of positively influencing the child's life altogether.

To summarize, the child therapist must be a relatively self-aware individual who is not afraid to seek help when she or he is faced with difficult situations, personal short-comings, or blind spots. The mental health professional who works with children must be extremely sensitive to cultural and gender issues and must not be rigid or biased in her or his approach. Flexibility and the ability to tolerate ambiguity and to adapt to changing circumstances are important traits of the successful child therapist. Finally, empathy and respect for both child and parent are crucial to ascertaining that therapy receives a fair chance at helping a child change.

CHAPTER THREE

COMMON REACTIONS
OF THE CHILD THERAPIST

CHAPTER THREE
COMMON REACTIONS OF THE CHILD
THERAPIST

Willingness to seek consultation is not reserved only for the therapist who has problems dealing with abusive or neglectful parents. Any therapist must keep an open mind about her or his work and must learn to recognize signs of when therapy is not working. Due to the multitude of issues that arise in work with children, it is the mark of a good therapist to seek consultation from a colleague when problem feelings are recognized. Countertransference and other emotional reactions in the work with children are unavoidable (cf., Webb, 1989). Surprisingly, however, this topic has received relatively little attention as compared to the frequency with which countertransference issues are discussed in the clinical literature in the context of adult therapy (Tyson, 1986). This lack of attention is perhaps due to the vast behaviorally oriented literature in the area of treatment of children. However, as Lanyado (1989) points out, regardless of whether a therapy approach utilizes the concepts of transference and countertransference in actual clinical intervention, they exist, and hence deserve to be defined, explored, and discussed. Such a discussion is necessary, as countertransference reactions are perhaps the single strongest contributor to treatment failures, more responsible for poor therapeutic work than either inexperience or lack of knowledge (Schowalter, 1985).

A Definition of Terms and Concepts

There are a number of reactions a therapist can have in response to work with children ranging from traditionally defined countertransference to inappropriate attachment to unhealthy identification. While the discussion of these processes perhaps appeals most to therapists and therapist trainees who have a theoretical orientation that is in the psychodynamic or psychoanalytic tradition, it is truly important that all child therapists at least read about these possible reactions. Nobody, not even the most symptom-focused clinician, can escape these responses or feelings altogether. Human beings respond to the plight of others, identify with them, react toward them, and perhaps even dislike them. In fact, "few clinicians would deny the obvious fact that they bring personal needs and expectations to their work, but therapists often 'forget' this when they should most keep it in mind, while they are doing their work" (Schowalter, 1985, p. 41). Only awareness that such reactions are possible before, after, and during treatment of the child and her or his family will help the child therapist maintain a therapeutic stance toward a client.

As the discussion here will point out, not all therapist reactions are negative in and of themselves. Some are positive feelings for the therapist, some are helpful to the child client, some facilitate the therapy process, and some actually ascertain that work can get done (cf., Schowalter, 1985). For ease of discussion and logical organization, reactions are divided into three categories: countertransferences, identifications, and attachments.

Countertransferences

Countertransference is most traditionally defined as a therapist's response to a client that is based upon the unconscious in general, and unconscious anxieties and conflicts in particular (cf., Freud, 1959; Webb, 1989). However, this definition is very global and does not differentiate the different possibilities that are contained within it. Hence, further definition is necessary to clarify four types of countertransferences that can occur in the treatment of children (see Table 3 for a brief overview). The first three tend to be more disruptive to treatment, whereas the fourth can serve a therapeutic purpose.

Issue-Specific Countertransference. The first type of countertransference will be labeled issue-specific countertransference for the purpose of this chapter. This countertransference represents a reaction resulting from the stimulation of unconscious material of the therapist in response to specific behaviors, feelings, and needs (or transferences) expressed by the child client. In other words, a therapist's reaction to a child's issues is flavored by the therapist's own unconscious material. For instance, a therapist who has anxieties about sexuality may be particularly threatened and may respond negatively to the discussion of sexual abuse by a young child client, especially if that child has learned and incorporated seductive behaviors. Another therapist who is free of unconscious sexual conflicts may respond to the same child in an entirely different manner. The therapist herself or himself may be very capable of treating other children, those who do not stimulate the therapist's sexual conflicts, without problem and very sensitively. The crux of this countertransference. is the coincidental and unfortunate coming together of therapist and client issues (or transferences) that are incompatible, too similar, or too threatening.

Stimulus-Specific Countertransference. A second type of countertransference, herein labeled stimulus-specific countertransference, is independent of the child's needs, feelings, or behaviors, but rather occurs in response to an external, therapy-irrelevant stimulus of the child. For instance, a therapist with yet-to be explored issues around sibling rivalry with a younger brother may respond with inappropriate interventions to those young male children who remind her or him of this brother. The reaction is not specific to the child's expressed therapy issues, but rather is specific to the therapist and would occur in the interaction with any such child, whether a therapy client or not. The crux of this countertransference is the therapist's unconscious and immediate reaction to an external stimulus that is independent of the child's treatment needs or transference expressions.

Trait-Specific Countertransference. Yet another countertransference reaction, herein called trait-specific countertransference, is even more global and has previously been labeled the therapist's "habitual modes of relating" (Sandler, 1975, p. 415, as quoted in Bernstein & Glenn, 1988, p. 226) or the therapist's "expression of character traits" (Lilleskov, 1971, p. 404, as quoted in Bernstein & Glenn, 1988, p. 226). Such a countertransference reaction implies that the therapist responds to the child client as she or he would respond to anyone and any time in her or his life. For instance, a therapist with rigid morals who tends to be condescending and judgmental in general, will bring this attitude into the treatment room and it will influence her or his work with a given child client, regardless of the issues presented by the child. Another therapist, who may detest aggression, may be unable to allow children to act out their own angry feelings, however justified they may be. The crux of this countertransference is the therapist's habit-driven manner of relating to children in all contexts, including the therapy setting.

Child-Specific Countertransference. Finally, the fourth type of countertransference is called child-specific countertransference. This countertransference is a reaction to the child that is solicited by her or him in most, if not all, adults with whom the child interacts. For instance, a very oppositional and demanding child with poor self-esteem and strong attention-seeking behavior may overwhelm and alienate adults after prolonged contact. The therapist may experience this same frustration others might encounter with the child. Hence, this reaction is not specific to the therapist's unconscious, but rather is specific to the child's behavior which solicits a given response in those around

Table 3

Definitions of Countertransference Types

Countertransference	Definition
Issue-Specific	the needs, feelings, or behaviors of the child are such that they stimulate a similar set of issues (or transferences) in the therapist; the reaction of the therapist to the child is now flavored by the therapist's own unconscious material
Stimulus-Specific	certain external, therapy-irrelevant stimuli emanating from the child, result in a response from the therapist that is based on unconscious conflicts and has nothing to do with the child's needs
Trait-Specific	the therapist has certain habits or character traits that are expressed in all interactions with children, including the therapy context, even if they are inappropriate for the client
Child-Specific	the child solicits a response in the therapist that is identical to the responses the child solicits in others

her or him. The crux of this countertransference is the child's solicitation of a consistent (e.g., negative, protective) response from her or his environment.

The child-specific countertransference, unlike the other three, provides the aware clinician with added insight about the child client and empathy for the adults in the child's life. Such a countertransference reaction can be used therapeutically with child and parents. It provides information about the child and can provide excellent feedback about the child's impact on the environment, as well as providing information about why this child tends to be rejected in many contexts. It also provides insight regarding target behaviors of the child that need to be modified quickly to help the child become more acceptable to the potentially helpful adults in her or his life. Finally, Lanyado (1989) refers to this reaction as an "in loco parentis counter-transference" (p. 99), suggesting that it provides an excellent means of creating empathy with a child's parent by being put in a situation that simulates the relationship between parent and child.

Clearly, while child-specific countertransference can be conducive to treatment, the other three tend to interfere or disrupt the flow of therapy. Intrusions based on the therapist's unconscious needs or general character traits result in the imposition of agendas that are not germane to the child, but rather meet the needs of the therapist. Self-reflection and self-awareness are important personality features of the child therapist, critical to the prevention of such negative countertransferences. It is not surprising that many clinical papers in the existing child therapy literature have called for therapists to have their own therapy prior to working with children. While this is certainly the best way of achieving clarification of how personal issues and habits can interfere with child therapy, knowledge of common negative countertransferences encountered with children can also be immensely helpful. Hence, below a number of common themes are addressed that tend to result in non-therapeutic treatment interventions and interactions between child and clinician. But first, definitions of two other common treatment reactions, identification and attachment, must be provided.

Identification

Not unlike countertransferences, identifications can have negative or positive effects on treatment, depending on whether they are processes emanating from the therapist and expressed without awareness, or whether they are processes emanating from the child and used consciously by the therapist. While identifications can have similar effects on child therapy as countertransferences, they are nevertheless different. There are two broad settings within which identifications can occur that are unique to the work with children. Specifically, only in the work with children can the therapist have a number of different identification reactions with two separate sets of players; namely, the child and the parent(s). In both contexts, two possible types of identification can occur. With the child, the therapist may experience identification or projective identification; with the parents, the clinician may experience identification or reactive identification (see Table 4 for a brief overview).

Identification With the Child. Identification with the child implies that the therapist has become so uniquely interested in and empathic with the child's situation that she or he identifies with it completely. The therapist feels for the child and understands the child from her or his unique perspective. So far this definition is strikingly similar to the definition provided for empathy in Chapter Two. However, identification takes the process of empathy one (unhealthy) step further. In her or his identification with the child, the therapist begins to relate to the child's environment as the child would. In other words, the therapist begins to relate to the child's parents through her or his identification with the child, not as a separate and objective other. The therapist may develop transferences and feelings for the parents that reflect those of the child, hence are likely to be immature and

Table 4

Definitions of Identification Types

Identification	Definition
Identification With Child	the therapist identifies with the child to such an extent as to approach her or his parents as if the therapist were the child; this confounds the parent-therapist relationship
Identification With Parent	the therapist identifies with the parent to such an extent as to approach the child as if the therapist were the parent; this biases the child-therapist relationship
Reactive Identification	the therapist dislikes certain aspects of the parent and begins to behave rigidly and biasedly in just the opposite manner from the parent
Projective Identification	the child projects an unacceptable affect or need onto the therapist who accepts as if it were her or his own without awareness that it originated from the child

biased. The therapist fails to see the parents' perspective and is likely to judge them harshly, subjectively, and unrealistically. In other words, through the identification with the child, the therapist loses her or his empathic stance with the parents.

Identification with the child can also result in regressive behavior and affect on the therapist's part (this process has also been called counteridentification; cf., Bernstein & Glenn, 1988). The clinician not only responds toward others as the child would, but becomes the child. Her or his interactions with the child begin to take place at the child's immature level of development and the therapist is no longer a guiding adult, but a fellow child, similarly unable to respond or deal with a given situation. The therapist may experience certain affects as overwhelming, much like the child with whom she or he is working, and her or his problem-solving skills become poorly defined and targeted. Such regression is also closely related to projective identification (see below). However, while projective identification can be used to enhance the therapeutic process (e.g., Brems, 1989b), identification with regression cannot.

Identification With the Parents. If the therapist experiences identification with the parents, on the other hand, the same process occurs, but in reverse. Now the therapist so non-discriminately empathizes with the parent(s), that she or he loses empathic track of the child. The therapist is now indeed in cahoots with the parent(s) and hence can no longer function effectively as the advocate for the child. Her or his alliances are with the adult and the child is left out in the process. This type of identification is quite dangerous in that it can result in the re-traumatization of the child who is in treatment subjected to the same attitudes and behaviors she or he experiences in day-to-day life from the parents.

Clearly, neither identification with the child nor with the parent is a desirable process. It results in biases and lack of empathy that can derail the treatment process regardless of with whom the therapist aligns. If she or he aligns with the child, the parents are likely to feel left out at best, attacked at worst. Either way, they tend to become less cooperative with treatment. Since they are in charge of payment and transportation, such a misalignment not infrequently results in premature terminations as parents withdraw their child from therapy. If the therapist aligns with the parents, the child is likely to resist therapy and may ask not to come back. If the child is forced by the parents to return (not an unlikely occurrence as the parents feel extremely supported by the over-identifying therapist), not only is treatment progress compromised, but the child may be re-traumatized. The therapist is likely to react with feelings similar to those of the parent and hence may become angry at the child if treatment fails.

Reactive Identification. Also somewhat destructive is the therapist's reactive identification with the child's parents. In this case the therapist disagrees with the parents and because of this disagreement, attempts to be different from how they are (cf., Bernstein & Glenn, 1988). The clinician may become extremely rigid and controlling if parents are perceived as too permissive or incapable of setting appropriate boundaries. Or the therapist may be overly permissive and tolerant of abuse by the child if she or he perceives the parents as controlling and emotionally abusive. Either way, the interactions between child and clinician are no longer determined by the child's needs and the therapist's therapeutic stance, but rather by the therapist's reaction formation to parental behavior. Such an approach cannot be successful as it neither provides therapeutic contact with a caring adult, nor a corrective emotional experience in a growth-promoting therapeutic atmosphere.

Projective Identification. Depending on the level of awareness about the process by the therapist, projective identification with the child can be positive or negative in its effects on treatment. In this scenario, the child attempts to get rid of an unacceptable or frightening affect or self aspect by projecting it onto the therapist. If the projection is successful, it will help calm and soothe the child as it serves to keep disturbing aspects of the self out of the child's awareness. The projection of the child is met by the therapist with acceptance and recognition or understanding, in other words, the therapist experiences the feeling projected by the child. If the therapist is aware that the affect she or he is currently feeling had its origin in the child and not in the self, she or he is capable of tolerating and altering it in some fashion that makes the affect more acceptable and bearable to the child. Once altered or metabolized, the affect is identified by the child as her or his own and is reintegrated into the self. This process of reintrojection is critical to the therapeutic impact of projective identification, as without the introjection, no change in the child can occur.

Without reintrojection, projective identification merely would have served as a defense in the same manner as pure projection. Without the metabolization of the projected affect by the therapist, reintrojection would not be possible in a therapeutic manner. The affect, unaltered, remains overwhelming for the child, cannot be reintegrated into the self, and continues to be rejected by the child. However, if the therapist is successful and accepting, recognizing and altering the affect, it will be acceptable to the child and can be incorporated successfully.

While this process sounds somewhat technical and abstract, it is actually a very experience-near procedure and always contains affective involvement on the therapist's part. It is this affective involvement that occasionally causes the cycle to derail and to end unsuccessfully. In other words, if the therapist 'receives' the affect but does not recognize it as the child's, rather perceiving it as her or his own, a projective counteridentification is set in motion. The therapist will feel overwhelmed or disturbed by the affect, cannot contain or alter it, and the therapeutic cycle cannot be closed. The therapist is left with feelings identical to those of the child and without recognizing that they originated in the child. Instead, the therapist accepts or perceives the feelings as her or his own, but is unable to deal with them.

Clearly, the projective identification process can be turned into a therapeutic experience for the child or it can serve to stifle the therapeutic process. It is a process that is particularly relevant to children as it is completely non-verbal and is actually used by infants to communicate affects to parents in order to have certain needs met (Klein, 1955). The process of evoking feelings in the therapist via projective identification is hence a nonverbal means of communication for the child (Lanyado, 1989). A child clinician must be particularly aware of such nonverbal expressions of affect by the child, as clearly lack of awareness hinders the therapeutic resolution of the feelings and needs. For more detailed discussions of the projective identification cycle, both positive and negative, the reader is referred to primary sources. The concept as applied therapeutically with children is presented by Brems (1989b, 1993), whereas application with adults is presented by Ogden (1982).

Attachment

Most, if not all, children stimulate attachment with the child clinician. Children who have traumatic histories of abuse or other types of suffering often evoke very strong attachment reactions from their therapists (Lanyado, 1989). Strong attachments to child clients are not bad in and of themselves. In fact, at times they are the only thing that protects the preservation of treatment under adverse circumstances. Specifically, many children with abuse histories can be very difficult to treat. Their behaviors may be out of control or they may present significant emotional challenges to their clinician. Having formed a strong attachment with such a child early in treatment may facilitate the therapist's ability to tolerate and endure negative interactions (including hostility, anger, and hatred) later in treatment, preventing premature terminations (Lanyado, 1989).

At times, however, overly strong attachments may interfere with treatment. It occur that child clinicians become so attached to their child clients that the emotional tie with the child overrides good clinical judgment. The therapist begins to respond from an emotional level, not a cognitive one, and relates to the child no longer as a client but as a love object. Such intense attachments can also lead to violations with regard to healthy therapeutic boundaries. The therapist may have the urge to help the child in settings other than therapy and may make unhealthy decisions about interventions in academic, home, or other settings.

An additional danger of attachment that has gone too far, is the possibility of the child becoming a "narcissistic extension" of the therapist (Bernstein & Glenn, 1988, p. 227). In other words, the therapist begins to use the child's reactions as a means of judging her or his own competence as a clinician. If the child behaves or feels well, therapy is viewed as progressing and the therapist feels positive about her or his role in the child's treatment; if the child behaves or feels poorly, therapy progress is assessed negatively and the therapist's self esteem and self confidence begins to falter. Clearly such attachments overstep the healthful boundaries of the child-therapist relationship and no longer facilitate treatment progress.

Discussion of Common Countertransference Reactions

So far, this chapter has presented general processes and definitions of reactions in the child therapist that can either derail or facilitate the therapeutic process. Now the chapter will turn to providing examples of specific themes or contents that are superimposed on the general processes outlined above. Most of the themes described here are most relevant to the context of the four types of countertransference. However, they can also contribute to identification and attachment process. A summary of themes is provided in Table 5.

Many therapists have chosen to work with children because of a special affinity they feel for this population. This special affinity can have many reasons, both healthy and unhealthy. It can also have many outcomes, again both healthy and unhealthy. Awareness of motivations for having chosen to become a child therapist and insight into one's own level of functioning are critical in order to avoid the themes that are presented. As will be detailed later, all of the themes described here are present to some extent in most child therapists. It is only if they become overpowering or replace other, more appropriate, reactions and interventions, that they become pathological or counterproductive to treatment.

Desire To be a Child Again

All adults, regardless of their level of satisfaction with adulthood, at one time or another muse about what it would be like to be a child again. This wish, however infrequently it normally occurs in the novice therapist's life, is not uncommonly mobilized in therapy with children. Childhood is usually viewed as an enjoyable time of life and especially therapists who may not have experienced childhood to its fullest, or who had parentified roles as children, will experience the urge to become children again. This urge is not a negative one if realized outside the therapy setting. Thus, child therapists not uncommonly find themselves loosening up in their lives outside the therapy room. However, if this desire carries into the room, it can prove counterproductive to the development of transferences and trust in the child-adult, client-therapist relationship.

The play in which child and therapist engage together can be very pleasure-producing for child and clinician. The interaction, especially if engaged in freely and happily, can provide an excellent backdrop for appropriate empathy and communication between child and therapist. Such an ability to "regress in the service of therapy" (Bernstein & Glenn, 1988, p. 231) is helpful

Table 5

Common Themes That Lead to Therapy Reactions in the Child Therapist

----

* wish to be a child again
* fear of being a child again
* wish to undo harm that was experienced by therapist as a child
* reemergence of own childhood trauma
* desire to be a caretaker or protector
* rescuer fantasies
* emotions in relation to the victim
* emotions in relation to the perpetrator
* themes surrounding the interface with the child's parents
* rigid adherence to a rigid theoretical system or intervention
* rigid insistence on a adult-versus-child distinction
* becoming the parent of the child, not the therapist
* fear of hurting child through confrontation or challenge
* teaching and playing with the child to keep her or him safe
* interacting with the child around didactic and instructional purposes
* need to be in control or in charge; commanding the child

----

and adaptive. But, if the therapist's behavior turns into a means of gratifying wishes and needs, the process becomes counterproductive. The therapist is likely to lose an objective approach to the child and while play still takes place, work is no longer on the agenda. At best, the child is having a fun hour; at worst, the child becomes a source of gratification for the therapist.

Fear of Being a Child Again

Quite to the contrary of the previous theme, some therapists become quite frightened by the playfulness and emotional flavor of the therapy session with the child. They become frightened of their own behavior, and even more so of their own enjoyment of the activities in which they engage with the child. This fear is usually fueled by a strong fear of regression that signals to the therapist (for whatever conscious or unconscious reason) the possibility of vulnerability. This vulnerability generally stems from the belief that play equals regression which in turn equals loss of control. Such loss of control is perceived by the clinician as the harbinger of poor coping and fragility of self-esteem (cf., Schowalter, 1985).

Undoing Personal Harm

The wish to undo harm that was experienced by the therapist as a child is another common theme that can lead to counterproductive therapy reactions on the part of the therapist. Not uncommonly, novice therapists express the desire, similar to new parents, to do something for their child clients that no one has ever done for them and to make sure that children now will be safer than children were when the therapist grew up. This countertransference can be dangerous for several reasons. First, it leads the therapist to make certain assumptions about the child that is being treated. The child is considered as representative of children in general, and of the child the therapist used to be, in particular. Thus, the child is not explored from her or his own perspective, but rather from the historical perspective of the therapist. This can lead to misinterpretations of the child's behaviors.

Therapists who are most vulnerable to this type of reaction are those who have entered the child therapy profession in an attempt to have their personal needs cared for. For these therapists, doing therapy with children is their personal attempt to have their own emotional needs met (Schowalter, 1985). Thus, assumptions are made about what the child client might need or desire based on the therapist's own needs and desires. Interventions will be patterned according to this understanding, regardless of whether it reflects the child's or therapist's reality. Many blind spots will enter into the treatment process.

Because of the therapist's needs and commitment to having them met once and for all, she or he becomes very committed to a positive treatment outcome. Much more hinges on the success of the treatment of this one particular child; the therapist's personal improvement is viewed (however unconsciously) as being at stake. The child case takes on symbolic dimensions and becomes a test case for the therapist's ability to fulfill her or his life goal of undoing harm of the past. Objectivity is lost and failure becomes overwhelming as it signals failure for the therapist at a very personal level.

Reemergence of Personal Trauma

Issues in the therapist's past may enter treatment via other avenues as well. Not all therapists who had bad childhood experiences enter the profession because they want to undo harm that was done to them. In fact, nothing may be further from the truth, as these therapists have convinced themselves that they have either resolved their childhood problems or had an idyllic childhood. If this conviction is based on denial or other defensive maneuvers rather than reality, dealing with a child's presenting problem may then lead to painful reemergences of the therapist's own childhood trauma.

Given that the clinician was not prepared for this reemergence as the trauma was believed to have been resolved, it leaves her or him stunned and in need of careful supervision or consultation. Reemergence must be dealt with swiftly for the sake of the therapist, as well as the child. It certainly may also occur in the treatment of adults, however, the identification with a child (as opposed to an adult) client makes the therapist more vulnerable. Not uncommonly does identification

65

with a child client take the therapist back to the developmental age with which the client presents, thus leaving her or him with the affects, needs, desires, and resources she or he had at that age. This young age results in feelings of being overwhelmed, frightened, startled; feelings that are not easily dealt with by the therapist alone.

Therapists not uncommonly react strongly to the child's parents, especially if abuse or neglect are part of the presenting picture. This reaction will be dealt with further below, but deserves mention here as well if the therapist was a victim of abuse or neglect herself or himself. Not only is reexperience a definite danger in this case, but so is the emergence of affects against the child's parents that are reflective of the therapist's affects against her or his own parents in childhood. Thus, interactions with the client's parents may become strained and confounded by the therapist's personal experience. As a positive relationship with a child client's parents is generally crucial to the continuation of the child's treatment, this countertransference may be particularly destructive if it leads to a breach in the relationship between therapist and parents.

Caretaking and Protection

Children also not uncommonly evoke the desire in the therapist to be a caretaker or protector (Thompson & Kennedy, 1987). Children are often viewed as vulnerable or powerless in their family systems. This perspective leads the therapist to the wish to safeguard and protect the child as best possible and to provide the child as much nurturance and protection during the therapy session as possible. The therapist fails to realize that this will not necessarily prepare the child to return to her or his non-nurturing environment.

One therapist who was working with a 3-year old child who was experiencing a particularly difficult divorce of her biological parents, was overcome with the desire to nurture the girl in treatment. She often emphasized the safety of the room and the therapeutic relationship and provided a very warm and cozy atmosphere for the child. The girl did appear to need this nurturance very much and certainly responded extremely well to it during the sessions. However, the approach failed to help her face the difficult parental situation in the home and provided her no new resources with which to protect herself once she left the therapy room. When she began to struggle more and more against ending her sessions, the trainee painfully recognized her role in this refusal of the girl to leave her at the end of sessions, and recognized that she herself often wished the session could continue. She was then able to move on to the use of several additional therapeutic strategies, such as mutual story-telling, to help the child build resources that could be carried beyond the walls of the therapy room.

Another danger of the protective role of the therapist is the tendency to avoid talking about or otherwise processing trauma (Thompson & Kennedy, 1987). The therapist may harbor the mistaken belief that the child cannot tolerate reliving the trauma and may, overtly or subtly, keep the child from processing what has occurred. Often this is a false protection, meeting the needs of the therapist more so than the needs of the child. Children need to process trauma they have experienced. This is not to be mistaken for the child's need to talk about the trauma or to discuss it with her or his therapist. Instead, the child may express and lay to rest traumatic experience through play.

Being the Rescuer

Working with children and their families often places the therapist in a situation in which a number of people look toward her or him to be wise, tolerant, and able to rescue them. This approach of some families and children to the clinician can lead to her or his desire to fulfill this expected role by becoming the person who will rescue the child and family from their own mistakes and inadequacies (Stadler, 1991). The therapist can live out fantasies of being competent and capable to make positive events happen in other people's lives. As many therapists enter the mental health field with the motivation to help others, the rescuer role is easy to accept, particularly if it is deemed desirable by the child.

However, as positive as the role may appear, it has many inherent dangers. First, despite the fact that it may have been elicited by transferences of the child and family toward the therapist, the therapist's actual acceptance of the role as rescuer only serves to reinforce for the child and her or his family that they are helpless and out of control. It suggests that the child and family are incompetent and may lead to feelings of humiliation and even rage (Webb, 1989). Further, the rescuer role gives the therapist a false sense of control and power that is likely to translate into self-righteous, condescending behavior, attitudes that clearly get in the way of empathic, caring, and respectful treatment.

Finally, being the child's or family's rescuer not only results in negative feelings toward the therapist by the family, but also tends to stifle the work with the child. It places a tremendous burden on the therapist who now feels that she or he has to meet all of the child's needs and has to help make up for past hurts perpetrated within the family (Webb, 1989). Such a burden is heavy to carry for anyone and may ultimately lead the therapist to resent the child and family or to end treatment prematurely because she or he begins to feel that nobody else is sharing the workload involved in the particular child's case.

Themes Surrounding the Interface with Parents

While the rescuer theme often occurs in the context of the child's family, it may be relevant also solely in the relationship with the child. However, a number of other therapy themes that result in unhealthy therapist reactions develop specifically out of the context of the interface role of the clinician between child and parents.

Some child therapists are prone to engaging in competitions with the child's parents (Webb, 1989).

They have made it their personal goal to be better than the parent and reflect an attitude that has been described as moral superiority and moral hypocrisy (Reynolds-Mejia & Levitan, 1990). These therapists tend to believe that they are better for the child than her or his parents, a stance that not infrequently leads to contempt for the parent (McElroy & McElroy, 1991).

Clearly, such a countertransference interferes with the establishment of a positive working relationship with the parents of a given child client. Parents tend to feel very vulnerable or defensive when their children are referred for therapy anyway. This defensiveness heightens their sensitivity to rejection, judgment, and contempt. If it is met by that very attitude on the part of the therapist, the relationship is doomed to failure. The parents, aware of the therapist's rejection and self-perceived superiority, tend to drop out of treatment before they have given it a chance to work.

Not only does competition with the parents affect the therapist-parent relationship, but it may also influence the therapist-child relationship and therapeutic process. Children identify with their parents and often get very attached to their therapist. If these two groups of people do not get along, the child is likely to get confused. Further, if the therapist gives subtle messages about the negativity experienced toward the child's parents, the child, feeling very much part of her or his parents, is likely to perceive this as personal criticism. Finally, children must be able to idealize their parents in order to derive the full benefit of the child-parent relationship. Messages from a therapist that these parents are somehow bad or inadequate undermines the possibility of a positive child-parent attachment.

Another reaction that tends to arise strictly because of interfacing with parents is the therapist's preconceived notion that the parent will interfere with therapy. Mild transgressions of boundaries (e.g., bringing the child to therapy with food because there was no time to eat at home), coincidental violations of limits (e.g., being late for therapy because of a snow storm) are interpreted by the therapist as treatment resistance and used as proof that the parent is not supportive of the child's therapy. The therapist will inadvertently or overtly express resentment to this parent. The parent, picking up the therapist's frustration and anger at her or him, is likely to feel guilty or to respond with hostility and anger in kind. Either way, a negative interpersonal cycle has been set in motion because of a therapist's habitual expectation that parents hinder their children's treatment.

A negative view of authority figures in general can also serve to confound the relationship with children's parents (Webb, 1989), leading to much the same results. Relatedly, some therapists are unable to see children's parents as mature and well-integrated human beings. Hence they tend to use splitting in their expectations. They tend to assign "good and bad images . . . to different parent figures, rather than integrat[ing both] appropriately within each" parent (Reynolds-Mejia & Levitan, 1990, p. 56). Such splitting can also occur with the child being pitted against the parent. Most commonly the therapist who engages in splitting will assign the child the idealized, good role; the parent the perpetrator, bad role. This results in denial of the good aspects of the parent and of the bad aspects of the child (cf., Hoxter, 1986).

Occasionally, the therapist will develop reactions to parents that are not at all negative, but rather are quite idealizing. The parents are seen as perfect human beings who have the sorrow and burden of dealing with a child who is identified as a 'problem'. Such an idealizing relationship with parents is equally harmful as a negative one. While it may facilitate the bond between therapist and parent, it interferes with the establishment of a therapeutic bond with the child. When there are two parents who are not in the same home, it is possible that the splitting mentioned above involves the idealization of one parent by the therapist and the perception of the other parent as deserving all the blame and responsibility for the child's problems. This can have grave consequences for the child, especially if the child is attached to both parents. The negative identification of one of the child's parents inevitable leads the child to feel rejected in the sense that she or he has incorporated aspects of both parents.

Emotions In Relation to the Victim

Certainly in the same context, therapist's reactions are particularly prone to countertransferential feelings if a family presents with the abuse of one of the children within it. Therapists tend to have strong feelings about victims and perpetrators and these attitudes are likely to emerge in their relationships with their clients.

With regard to the relationship with the traumatized child, therapists often feel a sense of inadequacy and helplessness as they often cannot alter the family environment for the child. Helplessness often leads therapists to engage in advice-giving and placating, superficial interactions that present an escape from the stifling feeling that comes from not knowing how to protect the child (McElroy & McElroy, 1991). Such a therapist may express sympathy rather than empathy toward the child in the attempt to protect the child from reexperiencing the trauma. However, a sympathetic, as opposed to empathic, response on the part of the clinician results in insufficient exploration and processing of the child's trauma. It merely falsely protects child and therapist from the painful and useful investigation of traumatic events (Reynolds-Mejia & Levitan, 1990). Rather than protecting out of a sense of helplessness and inadequacy, it is much more therapeutic for child and clinician to bring out the suffering.

Occasionally, therapists respond to traumatized children not with a sense of helplessness followed by the urge to protect, but rather with negative attitudes that hide the clinician's sense of inadequacy. Such therapists may engage in blaming and shunning, thus creating a distance between self and child (Hoxter, 1986). This type of response to a child's trauma is not only a reflection of unresolved issues about trauma on the part of the clinician, but also tends to re-traumatize

71

the child. Another negative therapeutic stance vis-a-vis victimized children, is the reaction to them as part-object. In this approach, the clinician is unable to focus on other aspects of the child besides the trauma. This reaction appears particularly likely if the child was traumatized such that physical disability has ensued (Hoxter, 1986). The clinician may get so caught up in the child's physical health and state, that she or he tends to ignore the rest of the child's being, losing track of her or his mind and spirit. Further, the clinician may focus therapy exclusively on the abuse.

Emotions In Relation to the Perpetrator

The response of the therapist to the parent of the victimized child is directly related to the therapist's response to the child. If the child is idealized, viewed as innocent and in need of protection, it is likely that the clinician will develop a non-empathic relationship with the perpetrator. She or he will exhibit a lack of sensitivity to the perpetrator's needs and historical context that might help explain (if not justify) her or his action (Reynolds-Mejia & Levitan, 1990). This parent is rejected by the therapist and through this action condemned to the greater likelihood of again becoming a perpetrator. The therapist's countertransferential inability to allow the abusive parent to vent and explore why she or he has developed abusive behaviors does not serve the child!

Quite to the contrary, some therapists who have a stronger alliance to adults may end up being very hesitant to believe in the guilt of the parent. Similarly, some therapists may have strong hesitations about confronting other adults about their behavior. However, and unfortunately for the child, "the unconscious resistance to confronting the adult offender, coupled with wishes for a close therapeutic alliance may lead the therapist to unwittingly protect and collude with the abuser or the non-protective parent" (McElroy & McElroy, 1991). This once again revictimizes the child and serves to perpetuate unhealthy interactional patterns. Clearly, given the consequences of both attitudes toward perpetrators, it is best if a therapist can be empathic and confrontive with both child and parent, intervening to protect when necessary and supporting when appropriate.

If the therapist responds strongly to a parent who is a perpetrator, care must be taken to watch for reaction formations (McElroy & McElroy, 1991). Specifically, a therapist, aware of her or his tendency to be harsh and judgmental about a perpetrator may react with sweetness and kindness, failing to confront the individual. This sweetness, however, was not fueled by true empathy and concern. Instead, it is a reaction formation expression of hostility and contempt. Similarly, the therapist who tends to collude with the abuser may feign confrontation. Again, this approach is not genuine and hence likely to be ineffective.

A final word of caution is necessary about the relationship of the therapist with adult partners of perpetrators. Care needs to be taken not to make quick assumptions about the non-protective parents. It is very easy to make a judgment that the partner knew about the abuse and failed to protect her or his child; however, there are some clinicians who argue that perhaps the parent was indeed innocently ignorant of what was going on (Gilgun, 1984). This caution certainly serves to reinforce the point that is being made here in general. The therapist cannot allow herself or himself to respond to either victim or perpetrator out of a habitual set of values. Instead, each individual child client and her or his family need to be assessed carefully so that any response to them on the part of the therapist is therapeutically, not countertransferentially, motivated.

In addition to the themes outlined above, Adams (1982) has identified and labeled six specific types of countertransferences that are common among child therapists, namely the True-Faith Healer, the Me Adult/You Child, the Good Enough Parent, the Big Sibling, the Baby-Sitter, and the Cop. While these tend to overlap somewhat with the themes outlined above, they deserve separate mention. In reading about these countertransferences, it is important to note that all of the approaches contained within them are appropriate to some degree and that they are not problematic in and of themselves. Thus, if the beginning therapist recognizes some of these traits in herself or himself, there is no need to panic because use in moderation of these approaches or affects may be quite useful. They become potentially counterproductive only if adhered to rigidly or if the therapist is unaware of their existence.

True-Faith Healer

The True-Faith Healer (Adams, 1982) holds the belief that there is one and only one appropriate therapeutic model and rigidly adheres to it regardless of how it meshes with the child's personality and presenting problem. This rigid approach forces the child's problem to fit into a preconceived mold, rather than exploring the child and her or his symptoms from a unique and individualized perspective. As pointed out previously, rigidity is not a desirable trait in child psychotherapy, and the therapist must be able to adapt treatment strategies to the unique presentation of the child and family. However, this is not to imply that the therapist must not follow a preferred theoretical system. Far from the truth; indeed, it is quite important that even the novice therapist have some preferred style or treatment approach. Flexibility comes from being capable to use a large number of strategies within the approach and compatible with it, to accommodate the needs of each client. Thus, even a psychodynamically oriented therapist will not shun other strategies if they are compatible with particular treatment goals, and may use reinforcers and extinction consciously and purposefully in the therapy process. However, the basic understanding of the child will be derived through a theoretical system in which the therapist believes. This belief, however, should never be pushed so far as to blind the therapist to the direct behavioral manifestations of the child's emotional difficulties. The

74

child should not be forced into a particular mold because of the therapist's beliefs. One must avoid the problem verbalized so eloquently by Maslow: "To those whose only tool is a hammer, every problem looks like a nail" (Adams, 1982, p. 40).

Me Adult/You Child

In the Me Adult/You Child Countertransference (Adams, 1982) emphasis is placed on adult-child differences through which the child is clearly disadvantaged because of less experience, less knowledge, and less power. In such a relationship, the development of trust is easily thwarted, and a relationship in which the child can be understood clearly from her or his perspective is never given a chance. Instead, the child is seen from a preconceived notion that she or he has no knowledge, no experience, and no power to contribute to the therapy process, in other words, is perceived as helpless and dependent. This approach not infrequently implies that the adult in the relationship felt this way as a child, and has learned to overcome or hide her or his feelings of powerlessness and helplessness through an identification with the aggressor, that is with adults in her or his childhood environment. Thus, her or his own adult behavior is driven not by mature adult feelings, but by the attempt to cover insecurity through firm, even aggressive, attitudes. In the therapy relationship, this type of adult-child relationship is counterproductive and fails to allow for adequate rapport.

Good-Enough Parent

The Good-Enough Parent Countertransference (Adams, 1982) is based upon the mistaken idea that doing therapy is like being a parent; that the therapist basically uses parenting skills that were learned and practiced on the therapist's own children, during the therapist's own childhood, or during her or his professional training. This belief can affect therapists with children of their own by making them feel more competent if their own children are well-developed and psychologically healthy, or incompetent if the therapists' own children are prone to having difficulties. Childless therapists who hold this belief feel incompetent, greatly disadvantaged, or unsure about their skills. However, nothing could be further from the truth than the notion that therapy is equivalent to parenting. Parenting is done on a daily basis; it envelops the child in a way therapy will never be able to. Yes, there are some parenting skills that translate into the therapy environment, but neither are they crucial to the building of rapport, not are they unique to adults with children of their own. In fact, more problems are encountered by therapists who have children and are very identified with their parenting role than by therapists who are not. For instance, one trainee who had four (very well-adjusted) children of her own frequently found herself cleaning up after her therapy clients, teaching, care-taking, and otherwise taking a mother role. She was painfully aware of this tendency and had great difficulty ridding herself of habits that become ingrained over 20 years of parenting. She had initially thought that her experience as a parent would greatly enhance her therapeutic interaction with children, but quickly realized that it more often than not got in the way. This is not to say that all parents will have difficulty being child therapists. Not so, they may merely need to watch this particular manifestation of countertransference more cautiously.

Big Sibling

The Big Sibling Countertransference (Adams, 1982) refers to the therapist who takes the approach that she or he is to become the big sister or brother for the child. In this approach, real therapeutic issues are avoided and merely a somewhat cautiously-guiding stance is taken. The therapist is reluctant to confront and challenge for fear that this may be painful for child. Focus of the therapy is on play only with the intent to provide a supportive holding environment in which the child can feel safe, yet somewhat intellectually stimulated. Thus, the child may be introduced to new games, new ways of dealing with stressful situations, new manners of playing with toys, even new problem-solving strategies, but process issues and history issues are never addressed. This therapy, while it is often engaging for the child, will remain superficial and will not explore problems in sufficient depth to create lasting change.

Baby-Sitter

Very similar to the Sibling Countertransference, the Baby-Sitter Countertransference (Adams, 1982) is focused on teaching and playing. In this approach, the adult feels entirely responsible for the child's welfare and change, as well as for all interactions that occur in the therapy. The child is seen as having been placed in the charge of the therapist who will watch over the child with a protective eye, but not necessarily with an eye that promotes self-awareness, psychological growth, change, or problem-solving. This type of countertransference is particularly common among novice therapists who are not clear about the purpose of therapy themselves, and who have not been able to identify process in treatment. It results in a fun-filled session for therapist and child after which the therapist cannot help but ask herself or himself what has been accomplished beyond keeping the child entertained and satisfied. Clearly, this is not the purpose of treatment, and such patterns must be addressed as they arise.

Teacher

The Teacher Countertransference (Adams, 1982) is similarly non-therapeutic in that it focuses on didactic, rational, and instructional purposes. While some instruction does and should occur in therapy, it is never to be used as the sole therapeutic strategy. Children cannot help but learn in treatment, and often rationality is an important aspect of intervention. However, there are many other components in the child-therapist relationship that are not present in the child-teacher relationship. For instance, the therapy relationship will be focused not on new knowledge acquisition per se but rather on self-awareness and growth. Strong emotions are often allowed to develop, and difficult aspects of the child's life need to be faced and dealt with. Material about the child's life might be shared to which a teacher would not routinely be privilege. Additionally, the teacher knows only limited parts of the child's life while therapists must keep abreast of as complete a picture as possible. The teacher-therapist also focuses so much on cognitive material that other human aspects are neglected. The expression of affect, the voicing of needs, and the sharing of desires may never take place. Instead, intellectualization, rationalization, and isolation of affect may be encouraged, which, in turn, further decrease expressed emotion in the child.

One trainee who had developed this type of countertransference frequently found himself helping the child with certain tasks the child had chosen for herself in the course of a session. For instance, one time, the young girl picked a floor puzzle that was in the therapy room mainly for assessment purposes. The child attempted to put the puzzle together, but frequently looked at the therapist to invite help. The therapist would respond to these looks by making suggestions about turning a particular puzzle piece or about trying a different place in the puzzle. When he was queried in supervision about the purpose of his behavior, he indicated he wanted to teach the child in a manner that would increase her cognitive complexity. While this is a noble goal indeed, it is not the therapeutic one that could have been followed up on in this context. For example, the therapist could have explored why the girl looked at him rather than openly asking for help, he could have continued to observe to see how she handled her frustration about being unable to complete the puzzle, or he could have addressed the idealizing transference that was developing in this therapy. Thus, a wealth of truly therapeutic information and opportunity for therapeutic intervention was lost through the didactic approach that had been chosen. The Teacher Countertransference is an easy one for the trainee to fall into as it is easily understood and implemented by the intellectualizing, bright adult that therapists often are. However, if the therapist finds herself or himself to be teaching and lecturing the child exclusively, a thorough look must be taken at the appropriateness of the overall treatment process.

Cop

The Cop Countertransference (Adams, 1982) reveals the therapist to be preoccupied with power issues, commanding the child and taking a shape-up attitude toward her or him. This therapist has the job of spelling out consequences and contingencies for behavior all the time at the exclusion of other therapeutic intervention. Again, in moderation this type of intervention is appropriate, but never as the only therapeutic strategy. Further, the preoccupation with power tends to get in the way of building trust, and the spelling out of contingencies and consequences makes it unnecessary for the child to figure these out on her or his own, or even ever to have to experience them. Sometimes trial-and-error learning can be very therapeutic for children and preventing this process is not always therapeutic. The cop-therapist also tends to be quite distanced and aloof, failing to allow the child to build a warm relationship with an adult in which she or he can safely experiment with new behaviors and affects. The aloofness of the therapist tends to squelch the expression of emotion and gives implicit messages about the inappropriateness of emotionality.

In summary, the common response themes and countertransferences discussed in this section and summarized from Adams (1982) are easy traps to fall into exactly because all of them include some behaviors that are occasionally appropriate in the context of therapy, just not to the exclusion of other means of relating and intervening! This list of countertransferences is by no means exhaustive, but merely meant to highlight the most common ones, and to warn the child therapist to be aware of her or his own unique reactions in treatment with children. Awareness of potential countertransferential feelings and attitudes will reduce (though not eliminate) the likelihood that they become counterproductive. In fact, occasionally countertransferential feelings can be used very effectively as meaningful therapeutic strategies, especially in the work with children.

This chapter was not written to frighten the beginning child therapist about the work with children. It has pointed out common reactions to child treatment in order to help the clinician become aware of the potential internal forces and overt behaviors that may result from the unique client that is the child. The message is not to fight against feelings that emerge in the treatment of children (Lanyado, 1989). Instead, becoming aware of feelings and responsive to all sorts of internal reactions and overt behaviors can help the therapist recognize important communications by the child and can point the direction for therapeutic interventions. Only if the therapist denies that she or he may have personal responses to the child client, will these reactions careen out of control and enter the treatment process in an uncontrolled and non-therapeutic manner.

CHAPTER FOUR

CHALLENGES IN DEALING
WITH A CHILD CLIENT

CHAPTER FOUR
CHALLENGES IN DEALING WITH A CHILD
CLIENT

Before the final decision about whether to embark on the psychotherapy venture with children is made, a few issues intrinsic to the process of psychotherapy with children and to the particular challenges children bring to treatment need to be highlighted. They are summarized in Tables 6, 7 and 8 and discussed here in detail. The prudent therapist must be aware of these challenges not only to make the decision to work with children, but also to enhance her or his ability to deal with these issues as they arise in the process of therapy.

Unique Issues Secondary to the Involvement of Parents in the Treatment of The Child

The term parent here is used in a wider sense of the word than usual. Specifically, it refers to the primary caretaker in the child's life, regardless of whether that person is biologically related to the child. As such, parents in this book are any adults who serve in a parenting role with a child, including stepparents, adoptive parents, foster parents, surrogate parents, and so on. Given this definition of the term parent, any time a therapist begins work with a child, the initial contact is made by a parent. A parent is in charge of bringing the child to treatment; a parent is generally in charge of payment; a parent usually is at least peripherally involved in the child's therapy. Given this reality, there are certain components in the treatment of children that arise specifically due to this involvement of a third party in the treatment of the client. In adult therapy, there is

Table 6

Challenges Secondary to the Involvement of Parents in Child Therapy

---

1. The child did not make the choice to seek treatment, hence may resist therapy.

2. The child does not know what therapy is about and hence may have unrealistic expectations.

3. The parent does not know what therapy is about and hence may have unrealistic expectations.

4. The parent may not know how to prepare the child for therapy and hence may need guidance.

5. The parents have right to be informed of their child's therapy, but the child's confidentiality must be honored in the process.

6. The child may reveal abuse or neglect by the parents necessitating reports to specific government agencies.

7. The child needs to be debriefed about any meetings between parent(s) and therapist.

8. The child may have a blended family, making it necessary for the therapist to interface and mediate with several adults in parenting roles.

9. The child may have several sets of parents who want to be actively involved in the therapy. Triangulation of the therapist may occur.

10. The child's therapy is dependent upon parents' collaboration regarding payment, transportation, and related issues.

---

rarely a third party whose involvement must be considered. Hence, the child therapist must learn what type of impact the parental involvement has on children's therapy and how to deal with it.

The Child as the Identified Client

Treatment of children presents many challenges that are not routinely encountered in the work with adult clients (Barker, 1990). Most importantly (because of its universality to all child clients), children rarely come to therapy on their own volition. Most commonly they are brought by a parent because of concerns of the parent about the child, or upon the recommendation of a teacher or school counselor. These reasons for seeking treatment can create unique resistances in the child for various reasons (cf., Klosinski, 1990). First of all, the child may perceive the therapist as being in cahoots with the parent or the teacher. Second, the child may perceive the therapist as intrusive and frightening because of her or his understanding of what the referral is all about. Not uncommonly will a therapist encounter a child who was threatened with therapy by a parent, in the sense of having been told that if the child does not change she or he will be taken to a therapist. This leaves in the child the expectation that the therapist is somehow going to punish the child or will require fast change and will side with the parent. If the referral was prompted by delinquency or acting-out, the child may be quite suspicious. These beliefs of the child may impede the development of therapeutic rapport and of therapeutic transferences and, therefore, must be addressed quickly by the therapist.

Child's and Parents' Expectations About Therapy

Related to the reality that they are rarely, if ever, the initiators of treatment, children often do not understand why they are taken to see a therapist, nor

85

do they usually know what therapy is all about. They may have all sorts of misconceived notions about what will happen to them and about the therapy process in general. In fact, one child who was seen in treatment was only told that he was going to see a doctor because of his bad grades. He was convinced that he would receive "shots" (having had a previous negative experience with inoculations), and was extremely frightened. Even though this fear was allayed immediately, he remained very hesitant during the intake interview and had great difficulty separating from his father for the individual child interview. Because of children's lack of knowledge about therapy, it behooves the therapist to talk about the reasons for and the process of therapy early in the intake interview. The therapist should invite the child to explore the process together and should address specific fears voiced by the child (Brems, 1993). Further, there are some very helpful children's books that are designed to prepare the child for therapy (e.g., Nemiroff & Annunziata, 1990). It is highly recommended to have such books available in the waiting room and to make parents aware of them when the first appointment is scheduled. In fact, parents should be strongly urged to discuss the decision to come to therapy with the child prior to attending the very first session.

Asking parents to prepare children, however, is often difficult because not infrequently parents themselves do not quite know what to expect from therapy, much less how to prepare their child. For this reason, the first telephone contact is best made by the clinician herself or himself so that this issue can be discussed with the parent. Specifically, the therapist can take this opportunity to inquire about parents' expectations about what therapy is like, and how it is hoped to help the child, as well as to tell the parents what therapy involves regarding time commitments, expenses, and length of treatment. Soliciting and providing this information allows the therapist to clear up misconceptions before the initial contact and lays the groundwork for helping the parent prepare the child.

It is good practice to ask parents how they plan to prepare a child for the first session. If the parents had no such plan, suggestions about what the child may need to be told can be made by the therapist. Such suggestions may include, but are not limited to, the introduction of the problem for which help is being sought, discussions of the difference between a therapist and a physician, the focus on talking and playing versus intrusive procedures such as inoculations or physical exams, the caring and nurturing position of the therapist as opposed to the punishing or challenging interaction that may be expected, the therapist's neutrality versus her or his expected alliance with the parents, the initial focus on the family rather than on the individual child, and the idea that the child will be asked to meet with this adult alone. Again, recommendations about and provision of references for preparatory books can be made at that time.

Parental Abuse or Neglect of a Child

The many possible countertransferential reactions a therapist might have because of parental abuse or neglect of a child was covered in detail previously. In addition of the stimulation of countertransferences, however, parental abuse also brings with it unique challenges to the treatment of the child. These challenges are legal and therapeutic in nature.

The legal aspects of child abuse are very clear-cut with regard to their definition and required action by law, but less clear-cut with regard to their effect on the therapeutic relationships involved. Specifically, while laws in almost all fifty states in the US clearly require that any suspicion of child abuse or neglect must be reported to the appropriate government agency (Zellman, 1990), therapeutic implications of such action have resulted in violations of the law by large numbers of clinicians (Bromley & Riolo, 1988; Kalichman, Craig, & Follingstad, 1990; Watson & Levine, 1989). Many therapists have argued that once a family is in treatment, therapeutic progress may be hindered, not facilitated, by current reporting laws. While this point is certainly arguable, the law is clear. Suspicion of abuse must and should be reported.

The consequences of this action can be ameliorated if the therapist engages in the action by involving the family and being sensitive to their needs and feelings. Thus, each child therapist needs to have a plan of action for interacting with a parent if a child reveals information leading to suspicions or evidence of abuse. Providing a step-by-step discussion of how reports can be handled optimally is beyond the scope of this book; the reader is referred to Brems (1993). Briefly, however, the therapist will best serve the child if, even in a situation of abuse or neglect, respect and caring are maintained vis-a-vis all family members. Confrontation, while necessary, is done respectfully and needs to include the parents in the process. One suggested plan of action is to convince the perpetrating parent to report herself or himself to the relevant agency in the presence of, with help from, and in addition to the clinician. Once the report has been made by parents and clinician, attention then has to be focused on re-establishing a therapeutic relationship with the family, protecting the child from harassment within her or his family, and continuing the therapeutic relationship and interaction with the child.

Parent Consultation About a Child's Therapy

Parents have a right to be informed about treatment progress and process of their children, if not only because they generally provide payment and transportation. These treatment updates must be done carefully, as they are necessary to keep parents informed, but must also honor the confidentiality of the child. There is often a fine line between divulging personal issues of the child versus providing evidence for movement and progress in treatment to the parents. It is generally best to focus update-sessions with parents on their perception of the child's behavior change and on process, as opposed to content, issues in the child's therapy.

Meetings with and involvement of parents may also affect the interaction of the therapist with the child. One 12-year old boy was quite uncommonly hostile in a session that immediately followed a meeting between his mother and therapist. When the therapist commented upon this, he disclosed that he was very upset about the meeting of the two women, as he was sure that they were talking negatively about him. This example demonstrates, that the therapist must be very sensitive to the child's suspicions and concerns about meetings with parents and should always discuss the occurrence of such a consultation with the child before and after it has occurred. If the child is old enough, and the parents sufficiently reasonable, it might be best not to meet with the parents separately, but to have a family meeting instead. This will demonstrate to the child that the therapist not only has nothing to hide from the child, but also honors the child's confidentiality.

Coordinating Multiple Sets of Parents

Even more challenging is the coordination of treatment and consultation when more than one set of parents is actively involved with the child. It is preferable to have conjoint sessions with all concerned adults; however, this is not always possible as the adults involved may not always be on speaking terms. Such a situation necessitates separate meetings with different sets of parents, and not uncommonly results in parents' attempts to communicate with the other set of parents through the therapist. Such triangulation is to be avoided, but at times may be necessary to ascertain optimal exchange of information among parents for the child's sake. The therapist must be very cautious about these issues and must be aware of the hidden demands placed upon her or him by the child's parents. The more communication can be facilitated among various sets of parents, the better for the child. Finally, it would be a grave mistake if the therapist ignored a set of parents who expresses the desire to be involved.

Cooperation of Parents in the Treatment of The Child

One final challenge that has to do with the fact that the client is a child, while not being caused by the child herself or himself, is that of the cooperativeness of her or his parents. Children cannot generally bring themselves to treatment; they depend upon the adults in their lives to do so. This fact often presents a great challenge for the child therapist because it leaves an important component of treatment under the control of a third party. Absences and tardiness cannot be interpreted in the same manner as with an adult client. Absences and lateness cannot be challenged with the child directly, and can be hurtful for the child and frustrating for the therapist. However, the worst of all decisions that parents can make in this regard are those related to the timing of terminations. Often treatment goals have not been entirely reached when parents decide that either enough progress was made to end treatment, or not enough progress has been achieved to date to warrant the hassles and expenses treatment involves for the parent. Terminations under these circumstances are not only obviously premature, but often painful and frustrating for both child and therapist.

Unique Issues Secondary to the Special Needs of the Child

Aside from special issue that arise because of parental involvement, there are also components of child therapy that render this process unique because of the special needs and features of children as a group. Children have different ways of expressing themselves than adults, often using verbal media significantly less. Further, their developmental level is vastly different from that of the therapist and may present a unique challenge to the mental health provider. Because of these differences, as well as because of children's uniqueness with regard to affective self-expression, therapists must be prepared to have more intense feelings in their work with children. This requires preparation in order to respond appropriately and therapeutically.

Table 7

Challenges Secondary to the Fact that the Client is a Child

----

1. The child communicates through a variety of meta-communications in addition to using language:
   a. metaphor
   b. symbolism
   c. play
   d. nonverbal communication

2. The child's developmental age is significantly different from that of the therapist, challenging the therapist to accommodate the child's special developmental needs in a number of areas:
   a. language and reasoning skills
   b. motoric development and needs
   c. sense of time
   d. emotional differentiation
   e. environment and equipment

3. Children express more intense and fluctuating affects and needs than adults, often leaving the unexpecting therapist startled or flustered.

4. Child clients tend to arouse more affect in the therapist than adult clients would.

The Use of Metaphor in Communication

Children communicate through metaphor and play, thus requiring the therapist to have some awareness and knowledge of ·· symbolism. Often, children communicate through comments or questions that, on the surface, appear unrelated to their presenting complaint. However, the therapist must learn to decipher their meta-communication. For example, one girl, who was seen in treatment because of psychotic symptomatology and a very deprived background, once asked the therapist in the course of play whether the cow she was using was going to have enough milk. The therapist, knowing the child's history, immediately understood her concern, which was two-fold. First, the child was asking if the therapist (whom she saw leave the play therapy room prior to her session with another child) would have enough caring and understanding to give for her as well as other children. Second, she was asking if her own parents were able to provide adequate nurturing and support for her. The therapist, with this understanding in mind, indicated that the cow indeed would have sufficient milk, though occasionally it may appear as though there was not enough to go around. When this concern returned at a later point in this child's therapy, the child learned through mutual story-telling what the calf could do for herself when the cow runs out of milk.

This example demonstrates not only the importance of understanding the metaphor, but also the need for the therapist to respond within the metaphor. Responding to the latent content by making it manifest (e.g., in this example by saying that the mother and father, or the therapist, will indeed attempt to provide for the child as best they can) can be much too threatening to the child. After all, there is often a reason why the child chooses the metaphor, and generally it has to do with the child's attempt at keeping her or his fear under control by addressing the issues indirectly or unconsciously. It is also important to remain with the child's choice of metaphor or language, that is not to introduce the therapist's own metaphor. The child may have difficulty understanding it, or may feel misunderstood by the clinician. While the novice may feel overwhelmed by the prospect of having to understand symbols and metaphors, this process is generally much easier than it sounds. After all, the therapist never enters treatment with a child blindly. Rather, she or he has in-depth knowledge about the child's dynamics and family situation, information gathered during the intake session (Brems, 1993). Having this context generally provides sufficient information to understand the child's symbolism. Further, children rarely use important symbols or metaphors only once. Thus, even if it is not understood the first time, there will be another chance.

It is important to keep in mind that each child will use symbols and metaphors in unique ways. Thus, what may mean one thing to one child, may have a totally and uniquely different meaning to another. The clinician should never assume that metaphors translate across children. Thus, studying symbolism (such as found in dictionary-type references that discuss the meanings of various story contents or objects) is generally not useful. It is much more productive to listen to the child's communication with an open mind and to place the play or verbalization in the context of the child's background and presenting concern. The same holds true for nonverbal communication, including body language. Behaviors or gestures are unique to each child and have specific meaning. For one child, lying down on the floor may indicate that she is beginning to trust the therapist, whereas for another child the same behavior may be a sign of resistance or avoidance.

For example, one child who was seen in therapy would take off her shoes at the beginning of the session as a sign that she was ready to get to work; when her session was over she would put on her shoes as a signal that she was reaching closure and was ready to end. Another child was observed to take off his shoes just like the first child. However, for him, taking off his shoes served a different purpose. He would routinely forget to put his shoes back on at the end of the session, thus having to return to the therapy room after having ended the session. Clearly, he communicated that he was not ready to conform to firm endings and beginnings of each session. Nonverbal communication is a powerful tool used by children of all ages. It must be considered by the aware therapist as a major means of self-expression, as well as a useful avenue for intervention.

Sensitivity to the Child's Developmental Level

Understanding the child's language and means of communication also fits into the larger context of adapting to the child's developmental level. The therapist must make efforts to be constantly aware of the child's cognitive level, and must have the ability to adapt to the child's way of processing information and self-expression (Bernstein & Glenn, 1988; Brems, 1993). This assumes that (as discussed previously with regard to educational background) the therapist has knowledge of developmental theory, as well as sensitivity to the special needs of a child that arise from this developmental context. To prepare the therapist for this task, her or his education must have addressed child development in detail.

While sensitivity to the child's overall developmental level is certainly the key to successful treatment, actual implementation techniques are beyond the scope of this book but can be found elsewhere (Brems, 1993). A few very common pitfalls will be discussed here.

Language and Reasoning. Most importantly, the child clinician needs to learn to adjust language used in the interaction with the child to the child's capabilities. Vocabulary may need to be scaled down, may need to be adjusted to specific regional variations, and may need to be expanded to include the language of the child's specific developmental stage (the latter is most relevant with adolescents). Communicating at the child's maturity level is critical. It is important neither

94

to over- or underexplain concepts. In other words, the therapist must take care to use language and reasoning skills that are neither too advanced nor too basic. The latter is often forgotten in the clinician's attempt to downscale her or his vocabulary or logic. However, treating all children to the same level of communication, whether they are three or ten can be perceived as insensitive, even condescending by the older child who has more sophisticated logic and language.

Motor Development. Another important aspect of development that is important to the child therapist is motor development. The child clinician has to adjust motor involvement to the child's needs (Lanyado, 1989). It is unrealistic to expect a young child to sit still for a long time. Children need to move around as they explore their environment and express themselves (Bernstein & Glenn, 1988). Hence, anyone considering doing child therapy must consider her or his willingness to be physically active and engage in physically challenging interchanges with the child. Even if not a lot of gross motor movement is involved, fine motor activities are highly likely. Finally, in the least, any child therapist must expect to sit on the floor, at least on occasion.

Emotional Differentiation. Another important consideration is a child's emotional differentiation. Young children do not yet have the skills of verbalizing emotions with regard to varying intensity and qualitative differentiation. Feelings tend to be global phenomena that change rapidly. A child clinician cannot expect an answer to questions that require the child to explain emotional experiences with regard to their subtleties. Children cannot tie more than one affect at a time to a given situation; they cannot explain nuances of affects felt in slightly different situations; they cannot recognize the simultaneousness of conflicting emotions (cf., Lane & Schwartz, 1987). Not being sensitive to these developmental realities can lead to inappropriate lines of questioning that are frustrating to both child and therapist.

Sense of Time. The therapist working with children must also be aware that children's sense of time differs from that of adults. "The child's sense of time is limited; [she or] he is conscious of the present and the near future, but the past and distant future make little impression. Hence, when the analyst suggests to a small child that [she or] he try to prevent future difficulties through analysis, the child may be puzzled" (Bernstein & Glenn, 1988). While not everyone may agree that the past makes little impression on the child, this quote is appropriate in its message that the child does not think in terms of yesterday and tomorrow. Her or his experience is much more bound to the present.

Additionally, for very young children, concepts of minutes and hours are vague. Thus, they are not served by statements that use these variables. For instance, if a 3-year old child asks how much longer a session will last, the therapist would not respond by giving a concrete time frame in minutes (e.g., we have 12 minutes) but rather would respond with a process statement that responds to the child's question (e.g., we have enough time left to finish what we are doing).

Environment and Equipment. A final developmental consideration is related to the size of the office used for child therapy and the equipment and furniture contained within it. A child therapy room should not be an adult office that is modified for an hour a week to accommodate work with children. It must be responsive to the child's smaller size, developmental needs for exploration, and reality that she or he needs to move a round and may touch things. A thorough discussion about child-appropriate therapy environments is presented in Brems (1993).

The Child's Fluctuations in Affect

Children who present for treatment are also often observed to have wide fluctuations in affect and behavior during their sessions (Bornstein, 1948). These may range from severe acting-out to significant expressions of depression. These quick fluctuations are often unnerving for the novice therapist who fails to consider that a child's reality is much more momentary and situation-bound than an adult's. The younger the child, the more likely that large fluctuations and strong expressions of situational affects occur. This is particularly true for the expression of negative affects which may be very intense at one moment, and completely denied the next. The therapist must learn to understand these fluctuations from within the child's developmental perspective to protect herself or himself from unnecessary frustration (Chethik, 1969). The therapist must also learn to live with the degree of unpredictability that arises from these wide fluctuations in the child's affects and needs states (Webb, 1989).

Additionally, children tend to express significant needs for dependency on their environment and the adults within it. Thus, they may make requests for help or support that tempt the therapist to provide for them. They may express significant needs that the therapist knows are not met by parents. These situations are taxing for the therapist, often leaving her or him feeling helpless and uncaring. For instance, one therapist who was working with a 4-year old child who had to leave her family for the summer and was very distraught by this fact, found himself feeling both angry and very helpless. He began to doubt the value of the treatment and became the victim of his own sense of not being able to help and to let the child depend on him for help. He had to come to terms with his own helplessness before he could help this child master hers, and help her ready herself for the summer without her family by using imagery and other visualization strategies that would help her gain a sense of permanence of the existence of her psychological parents.

The Therapist's Evoked Feelings

Children, in addition to expressing affect more intensely and with more variability than adult clients, also tend to arouse more emotion in the therapist than do adult clients. These feelings can range from aggression to protectiveness to fear to tension and to out-of-control feelings. Unless the therapist is prepared for this affect she or he may easily be overwhelmed by it. Dealing with a child with a horrendous abuse history is very taxing and draining and requires good mental preparation on the therapist's part. In fact, some children are best seen with no appointment scheduled immediately after the session because of the emotional impact the session can have on the therapist. This might appear like quite an unaffordable luxury to the therapist; however, it may prove to be a necessity in terms of ascertaining that the next client being seen receives the full benefit of a well-functioning therapist. If schedule flexibility cannot be arranged, this child should be the last client the therapist plans to see for that particular day. Fortunately, not many children are so taxing that this is necessary.

In summary, the challenges children bring to treatment by virtue of being children are difficult for the novice. They are best mastered through practice and experience. This experience can be gained from observing supervisors or colleagues conducting sessions, and discussing them afterwards. Further, they are challenges that are difficult for adults because they reflect what is so uniquely true for children. Children have not yet forgotten that language is not the only means of communication, and they make use of avenues for self-expression that many adults have lost. They are still willing to give their creativity free rein and are much less inhibited. There is much to learn from this creativity and freedom expressed by children, not only for the benefit of conducting better treatment, but also for some very personal beneficial side effects for the novice therapist. As one trainee pointed out, working with children made her increasingly aware of adults' meta-communication and gave her new respect for the usefulness of play and playfulness. Her work with children subsequently improved her work with adults, as well as her own self-awareness.

Unique Issues Secondary to the Process of Child Therapy

Not only does the child client per se hold unique challenges, but the entire process of the treatment of a child client has features that are distinct from therapy with adults. While these features are consequences of the fact that the client is a child, they are worthy of being considered as separate issues. The issues are listed here, but specific solutions are beyond the scope of this book. The reader is responsible for finding this information elsewhere (e.g., Brems, 1993).

Personal Questions

Therapists who work with adults are aware that many questions asked by adult clients have both a surface and a process meaning. For instance, questions about the therapist's preferences with regard to certain issues may be mere curiosity on the surface, but may represent an issue of trust and confidence on the part of the client in the therapist on a process level. The necessity to evaluate questions not only on the surface, but also with regard to process is especially important in the work with children. Children have their own unique way of interviewing the therapist and have a way of asking loaded questions that may be easily mistaken for direct curiosity about the therapist, therapy process, or the play therapy room. There are two major types of loaded questions. One has to do with information solicited about the therapist herself or himself, or deals with the relationship that is being forged between the child and the therapist. The other has to do with therapy process issues and with resistances, fears, or defenses that the child has mobilized in the treatment room. Both generally reflect a particular type of transference that is developing in the child toward the therapist, and both must be understood and addressed, if not answered, within that context. For a thorough discussion about how to deal with personal questions, the reader must read other sources (Brems, 1993).

Table 8

Challenges Secondary to the Process of Child Therapy

----

1. The child tends to ask loaded questions that need to be explored for underlying content. Often these questions deal with:
    a. personal information about the therapist
    b. therapy process issues and resistances

2. The child is more likely than the adult client to make requests for gifts or to bring small gifts to the therapist.

3. The child client is likely to initiate physical touch and affection at a higher rate than the adult client. The therapist needs to be prepared to address this issue and respond appropriately.

4. The child client at times requests to engage in therapy outside the therapy room. The therapist must make therapeutic decisions in those circumstances.

5. The child client is more likely than the adult client to flee the therapy room if difficult treatment issues have emerged. Safety is a crucial issue that determines the therapist's preparation and response.

Requesting and Presenting Gifts

Children, more often than adults, will bring gifts or ask to receive gifts from the therapist. While the issue of gifts is controversial and addressed in many different ways from clinician to clinician, it is important to consider it anew in relation to child clients. Perhaps the best approach is not to give gifts, except under exceptional circumstances. For instance, small gifts may be made as a sign of appreciation at termination. Sometimes, small gifts are appropriate as transitional objects if a lengthy break in treatment is anticipated, such as due to a vacation. Gifts should never be given to the child as a sign of caring or concern. These feelings are best expressed through actions. Further, children may also be allowed to take home with them the creations they produced during their session, such as drawings or other art objects. However, the initiative for such action must come from the child; the therapist should never prompt or ask the child to take these items home. In fact, some children are quite insistent that the therapist keep these items in a safe place so the child may use them or see them again later in treatment.

Receiving gifts is a much more difficult matter. Children do not give expensive gifts; thus, the therapist is rarely ethically obligated to refuse them. Gifts brought by children often are self-created items of art, drawings, or food. The therapist must attempt to recognize the meaning of the gift and communicate this understanding. Thus, a drawing may be accepted by the therapist, indicating that the therapist is very happy to see that the child is creative outside the therapy room and thinks about the therapy and clinician while at home. Items of food should be shared with the child in the session, acknowledging that the therapist understands that the child feels very nurtured and cared for by the therapist. In the treatment of one 7-year old girl, her offering of cookies to the therapist was a significant turning-point in her treatment. She originally had great difficulty attaching to the therapist, having experienced many short-lived and rejecting relationships in her life. As she became more comfortable in therapy, she often sought physical contact from the clinician, revealing her great need for protection and nurturance. Over the course of several months, she slowly began to feel more confident about her own ability to care for herself and to feel strong. Her gift of food at this time was interpreted as her way of communicating to the therapist that she was ready to nurture herself and to begin thinking about termination.

Physical Touch and Affection

Children are more likely than adults to express their affection or gratitude through physical means. While touch is rarely an issue in adult therapy, it is important to consider in a child's treatment. The child clinician cannot assume that all children enjoy or desire physical touch. Some children, especially children with abusive backgrounds may be fearful of touch. Other children, may want it very much and interpret a therapist's resistance to touch as rejection. Regardless of how the child feels about touch, if a therapist uses touch regularly, she or he should let the child's parent(s) know of this means of relating. Parents who were not told that touch may be involved, might get suspicious or angry about reports by their children of physical affection between child and therapist.

With regard to whether touch is used, the therapist must let the child take the lead. If a child touches, touch by the therapist might be appropriate. Of course this touch should never be sexual; however, fear of touch being interpreted in a sexualized manner by another adult should not hinder the therapist from using it if a therapeutic reason exists. If touch is used in therapy, the therapist must take care that it is not uncomfortable for the child. Further, if touch had to be used with a child for restraining purposes, it should also be used in more positive ways to communicate to the child that touch is not always bad or negative.

Other Common Child Therapy Process Issues

Given their greater activity level, it is not surprising that children often make requests for therapy outside the therapy room. This is indeed a request that appears to be unique to children; adult clients usually appreciate the confidentiality the therapy room provides. Children are less likely to be concerned with this. Their need to move about often is great. However, at times children do make requests that are indeed indicative of resistance or avoidance. The request to leave the room is one of these. It is much harder to focus on a specific, self-expressive or therapeutic activity outside the confines of the safe haven of the therapy room. It is much less likely that close interactions between child and therapist can take place. Hence, while these requests occasionally may be made, the therapist in general does not grant them.

On occasion, a child may be confronted with feelings of such intensity, that her or his desire to avoid them may move beyond a mere request for leaving the room. The child may actually attempt to escape from the office. An adult client will rarely if ever act upon such an impulse to get away. A child, however, being much more spontaneous in behavior, might. This reality has implications for clinic lay-out, as well as therapist behavior. Being prepared is the best caution against losing control of a therapy situation.

Relatedly, children are more likely than adults to act out behaviorally in the therapy room. Several cautionary, or safety, limits must be set with children. If acting out occurs that threatens the safety of the child, the therapist or the equipment, firm limits must be set and enforced. Again, the reader is referred to Brems (1993) for specific intervention recommendations.

In summary, the challenges of child therapy are many, but none is insurmountable. Most can be easily tackled if the therapist is well prepared, willing to be flexible, and able to allow herself or himself to follow a child's lead. In fact, often it is the very challenging nature of child therapy that can make it so exciting and gratifying. Therapy challenges that face the child therapist keep her or him alert, young, sensitive, respectful, aware, and active. What better way to keep growing as an individual than by helping a child?

**SUMMARY AND
CONCLUDING THOUGHTS**

WHERE TO GO FROM HERE

SUMMARY AND CONCLUDING THOUGHTS
WHERE TO GO FROM HERE

At this point the novice clinician should have become aware of the multitude of issues that one needs to be knowledgeable and skilled about before entering into treatment with a child client. The type of relationship adults tend to forge with children, the special circumstances children bring to treatment, and the unique process issues that are intrinsic to the work with them, present extraordinary challenges in child psychotherapy. However, with self-awareness and the willingness to maintain an open mind and seek consultation, the work with children can indeed be one of the most gratifying experiences for a therapist. As these issues were introduced here merely to give the trainee a basis for making a decision regarding the work with children, those readers who by now have decided to take the challenge and begin work with children must next turn to more detailed readings about the specific process of child therapy. While many books exist that tackle this content, the current book was written to prepare the reader for the use of *A Comprehensive Guide to Child Psychotherapy* (Brems, 1993).

This guide provides a step-by-step introduction to the therapeutic work with children. It is uniquely designed to present a comprehensive interpersonal, systemic-psychodynamic approach to psychotherapy with children age three years to approximately twelve years. It discusses psychotherapy with children for novices and advanced professionals in the mental health field, thus provides thorough introductions, definitions of key concepts, and outlines to simplify and clarify material. While it takes a interpersonal, systemic-psychodynamic conceptual approach, it integrates a number of techniques that need not be theory-bound.

107

The *Comprehensive Guide to Child Psychotherapy* was developed with the beginning child psychotherapist in mind. Nevertheless, its approach is conceptually complex and integrative, and yet simple and general enough to be easily understandable. The outline of the book is such that it parallels the process of work with children. First, it helps the beginning therapist understand the requirements of the environment in which child psychotherapy takes place, then it prepares the therapist for this work through discussion of ethics, development, and cultural issues in child therapy. In its second section, the book walks the beginning child therapist through the initial stages of intake, assessment, and conceptualization before moving on to therapeutic issues. Then it focuses on the therapeutic process and specific techniques in the middle stages of psychotherapy. It ends with a thorough discussion of termination issues.

The *Comprehensive Guide to Child Psychotherapy* makes use of many features that facilitate learning, including chapter summaries, tables, illustrations, and bibliographies. It relies upon case material to support conceptual points and to demonstrate clinical techniques. It minimizes jargon, and maximizes explanation and illustration. It represents an attempt at integrating interpersonal, systemic-psychodynamic case conceptualization with numerous techniques, including behavioral strategies, art, story-telling, and parent education. While combining strategies of these diverse approaches may sound incompatible upon first reading, it is actually a preferable way of conducting child psychotherapy. Literature exists that is supportive of psychodynamic and behavioral approaches, and clinical experience has demonstrated that a combination of the two schools of thought is highly successful in creating change in children. Specifically, a comprehensive and integrating approach will avoid the mistake of disregarding important features in a child's life. Strict adherence to one approach of looking at children is simplistic and disregards the realities of modern life. Children rarely grow up in the vacuum of a nuclear family anymore, nor is the family an easily-understood system.   Children are profoundly impacted by their larger environments and culture, and all of these factors must be considered.   Similarly, children are not merely the product of cause-and-effect or reinforcement contingencies.   Human interactions are much more complex than such a strict behavioral approach would suggest.   Nevertheless, behavioral strategies are a critical piece of intervention with children.

Reading this suggested text or any of the other existing child psychotherapy books will put the novice therapist well on her or his way toward experiencing the enjoyment that comes from working with children.

REFERENCES

REFERENCES

Adams, P.L. (1982). A primer of child psychotherapy (2nd Ed.). Boston: Little, Brown, & Company.

American Psychological Association (1973). Guidelines for psychologists conducting growth groups . American Psychologist, 28, 933.

American Psychological Association (1978). Principles concerning the counseling and therapy of women. Counseling Psychologist, 7(4), 74-76.

American Psychological Association (1981). Speciality guidelines for the delivery of services by clinical (counseling, industrial/organizational, and school) psychologists. American Psychologist, 36, 639-681.

American Psychological Association (1985). Standards for educational and psychological testing. Washington, DC: Author.

American Psychological Association (1987). General guidelines for providers of psychological services. American Psychologist, 42, 712-723.

American Psychological Association. (1987). Resolutions approved by the National Conference on Graduate Education in Psychology. American Psychologist, 42, 1070-1084.

Ammerman, R.T., & Hersen, M. (1992). Assessment of family violence: A clinical and legal source book. New York: Wiley.

Axline, V. (1947). Play therapy. Boston: Houghton Mifflin

Barker, P. (1990). Clinical interviews with children and adolescents. New York: W.W. Norton & Company.

Barrett-Lennard, G. (1981). The empathy cycle: Refinement of a nuclear concept. Journal of Counseling Psychology, 28, 91-100.

113

Berman, A.L. (1990). Standard of care in assessment of suicide potential. Psychotherapy in Private Practice, 8, 35-41.

Bernstein, I., & Glenn, J. (1988). The child and adolescent analyst's emotional reactions to his patients and their parents. International Review of Psycho-Analysis, 15, 225-241.

Bjorklund, D.F. (1989). Children's thinking: Developmental function and individual differences. Pacific Grove, CA: Brooks/Cole.

Bornstein, B. (1948). Emotional barriers in the understanding and treatment of young children. American Journal of Orthopsychiatry, 18, 691-697.

Brems, C. (1989a). Dimensionality of empathy and its correlates. Journal of Psychology, 123, 329-337.

Brems, C. (1989b). Projective identification as a self psychological change agent in the psychotherapy of a child. American Journal of Psychotherapy, 43, 598-607.

Brems, C. (1993). A comprehensive guide to child psychotherapy. Boston: Allyn & Bacon.

Brems, C., Baldwin, M., & Baxter, S. (1993). Empirical evaluation of a self-psychologically oriented parent education program. Family Relations, 42, 26-30.

Bromley, M.A., & Riolo, J.A. (1988). Complying with mandated child protective reporting: A challenge for treatment professionals. Alcoholism Treatment Quarterly, 5, 83-96.

Chess, S., & Hertzig, M.E. (1991). Annual progress in child psychiatry and child development. New York: Brunner/Mazel.

Chethik, M. (1969). The emotional wear and tear of child therapy. Smith College Studies in Social Work, February, 147-156.

Chrzanowski, G. (1989). The significance of the analyst's individual personality in the therapeutic relationship. Journal of the American Academy of Psychoanalysis, 17, 597-608.

Chung, C. (1990). Psychotherapist and expansion of awareness. Psychotherapy and Psychosomatics, 53, 28-32.

Coppolillo, H.P. (1987). Psychodynamic psychotherapy of children. Madison, CT: International Universities Press.

Dillard, J.M. (1983). Multicultural counseling: Toward ethnic and cultural relevance in human encounters. Chicago: Nelson-Hall.

Erikson, E. (1950). Childhood and society. New York: Norton.

Fauber, R.L., & Kendall, P.C. (1992). Children and families: Integrating the focus of interventions. Journal of Psychotherapy Integration, 2, 107-123.

Freud, S. (1952). A general introduction to psychoanalysis. New York: Pocket Books.

Freud, S. (1959). The future prospects of psychoanalytic therapy. In E. Jones (Ed.), Collected papers (Vol. 2, pp. 285-296). New York: Basic.

Gerrity, K.M., Jones, F.A., & Self, P.A. (1983). Developmental psychology for the clinical child psychologist. In C.E. Walker & M.C. Roberts, (Eds.), Handbook of Clinical Child Psychology (pp. 47-72). New York: John Wiley and Sons.

Gibbs, J.T., & Huang, L.N. (Eds.). (1989). Children of color: Psychological interventions with minority youth. San Francisco: Jossey-Bass.

Gilgun, J.F. (1984, Fall). Does the mother know? Alternatives to blaming mothers for child sexual abuse. Response, pp. 2-4.

Ginott, H.G. (1964). Problems in the playroom. In M.R. Haworth (Ed.), Child psychotherapy. New York: Basic Books.

Graham, S.A. (1980). Investigation of therapists' attitudes toward offender clients. Journal of Consulting and Clinical Psychology, 48, 796-797.

Hoxter, S. (1986). The significance of trauma in the difficulties encountered by physically disabled children. Journal of Child Psychotherapy, 12, 87-102.

Johnson, M.E. (1993). A culturally sensitive approach to therapy with children. In C. Brems, A comprehensive guide to child psychotherapy (pp. 68-93). Boston: Allyn & Bacon.

Kagan, J., & Lamb, S. (1987). The emergence of morality in young children. Chicago: University of Chicago Press.

Kalichman, S.C., Craig, M.E., & Follingstad, D.R. (1990). Professionals' adherence to mandatory child abuse reporting laws: Effects of responsibility attribution, confidence ratings and situational factors. Child Abuse and Neglect, 14, 69-77.

Keinan, G., Almagor, M., & Ben-Porath, Y.S. (1989). A reevaluation of the relationship between psychotherapeutic orientation and perceived personality characteristics. Psychotherapy, 26, 218-226.

Klein, M. (1955). On identification. In M. Klein, Envy and gratitude and other works, 1946-1963 (pp. 141-175). New York: Delacorte Press/Seymour Laurence.

Klosinski, G. (1990). Questions of guidance and supervision at the beginning of psychotherapy in children and adolescents. Psychotherapy and Psychosomatics, 53, 80-85.

Knobel, M. (1990). Significance and importance of the psychotherapist's personality and experience. Psychotherapy and Psychosomatics, 53, 58-63.

Kohut, H. (1984). How does analysis cure? Chicago: International Universities Press.

Kohut, H., & Wolf, E. (1978). Disorders of the self and their treatment. International Journal of Psychoanalysis, 59, 413-425.

Kolevzon, M.S., Sowers-Hoag, K., & Hoffman, C. (1989). Selecting a family therapy model: The role of personality attributes in eclectic practice. Journal of Marital and Family Therapy, 15, 249-257.

Kupfermann, K., & Smaldino, C. (1987). The vitalizing and revitalizing experience of reliability: The place of touch in psychotherapy. Clinical Social Work Journal, 15, 223-235.

Lane, R.D., & Schwartz, G.E. (1987). Levels of emotional awareness: A cognitive-developmental theory and its applications to psychopathology. American Journal of Psychiatry, 144, 133-143.

Lanyado, M. (1989). Variations on the theme of transference and countertransference in the treatment of a ten year old boy. Journal of Child Psychotherapy, 15, 85-101.

Lerner, R.M., Skinner, E.A., & Sorrell, G.T. (1980). Methodological implications of contextual/dialectic theories of development. Human Development, 23, 225-235.

Lewis, K.N., & Walsh, W.B. (1980). Effects of value-communication style and similarity of values on counselor evaluation. Journal of Counseling Psychology, 27, 305-314.

McElroy, L.P., & McElroy, R.A. (1991). Countertransference issues in the treatment of incest families. Psychotherapy, 21, 48-54.

Moss-Kagel, C., Abramovitz, R., & Sager, C.J. (1989). Training therapists to treat the young child in the family and the family in the young child's treatment. Journal of Psychotherapy and the Family, 5, 117-144.

Muslin, H.L., & Val, E.R. (1987). The psychotherapy of the self. New York: Brunner/Mazel.

Nemiroff, M.A., & Annunziata, J. (1990). A child's first book about play therapy. Washington, DC: American Psychological Association.

Ogden, T.H. (1982). Projective identification and psychotherapeutic technique. New York: Jason Aronson.

Piaget, J. (1967). Genesis and structure in the psychology of intelligence. In D. Elkind (Ed.), Six psychological studies by Piaget. Chicago: Random House.

Poal, P., & Weisz, J.R. (1989). Therapists' own childhood problems as predictors of their effectiveness in child psychotherapy. Journal of Clinical Child Psychology, 18, 202-205.

Reynolds-Mejia, P., & Levitan, S. (1990). Countertransference issues in the in-home treatment of child sexual abuse. Child Welfare, 69, 53-61.

Schowalter, J.E. (1985). Countertransference in work with children: Review of a neglected concept. Journal of the American Academy of Child Psychiatry, 25, 40-45.

Schweid, E.I. (1980). Sex bias in child therapy. American Psychologist, 35, 681-682.

Siegel, H.B. (1990). Working with abrasive patients. Issues in Ego-Psychology, 13, 48-53.

Skidmore, S.L. (1990). Suggested standards for child abuse evaluations. Psychotherapy in Private Practice, 8, 23-33.

Stadler, A.E. (1985). Die Begegnung des Therapeuten mit seinem kindlichen Patienten in der analytischen Spieltherapie. Zeitschrift fuer Individualpsychologie, 10, 184-193.

Stadler, A.E. (1991). Die Initialphase in der analytischen Psychotherapie mit Kindern und Jugendlichen. Zeitschrift fuer die Individualpsychologie, 16, 267-273.

Stern, D.N. (1977). The first relationship: Infant and mother. Cambridge, MA: Harvard University Press

Stern, D.N. (1985). The interpersonal world of the infant. New York: Basic Books.

Stern, D.N. (1989). The representation of relational patterns. In A.J. Sameroff & R.N. Emde (Eds.), Relationships and relationship disorders. New York: Basic Books.

Thompson, C.L., & Kennedy, P. (1987). Healing the betrayed: Issues in psychotherapy with child victims of trauma. Journal of Contemporary Psychotherapy, 17, 195-202.

Tuma, J.M. (1989). Specialty training issues for independent practice. Psychotherapy in Private Practice, 7, 75-84.

Tyson, R.L. (1986). Countertransference evolution in theory and practice. Journal of the American Psychoanalytic Society, 34, 251-274.

Watson, H., & Levine, M. (1989). Psychotherapy and mandated reporting of child abuse. American Journal of Orthopsychiatry, 59, 246-256.

Webb, N.B. (1989). Supervision of child therapy: Analyzing therapeutic impasses and monitoring countertransference. The Clinical Supervisor, 7, 61-76.

Weisz, J.R., Weiss, B., Alicke, M.D., & Klotz, M.L. (1987). Effectiveness of psychotherapy with children and adolescents: A meta-analysis for clinicians. Journal of Consulting and Clinical Psychology, 55, 542-549.

Whitehurst, G.J. (1982). Language development. In B.B. Wolman (Ed.), Handbook of developmental psychology. Englewood Cliffs, NJ: Prentice Hall.

Wilcox, B.L., & Naimark, H. (1991). The Rights of The Child: Progress toward human dignity. American Psychologist, 46, 49-52.

Zellman, G.L. (1990). Child abuse reporting and failure to report among mandated reporters. Journal of Interpersonal Violence, 5, 3-22.